opqrstuvwxyz
OPQRSTUVWXYZ

Bell & Hyman
First Colour
DICTIONARY

Robin Hyman
Pictures by Mary Budd

Bell & Hyman

Published in 1985 by
Bell & Hyman Limited
Denmark House
37–39 Queen Elizabeth Street
London SE1 2QB

British Library Cataloguing in Publication Data

Bell & Hyman First Colour Dictionary.
  1. English language–Dictionaries, Juvenile
I. Hyman, Robin
  423   PE1628.5

ISBN 0-7135-1441-8
ISBN 0-7135-1428-0 Pbk

Typeset in 11/11½ Linotron Century Schoolbook by
Tradespools Limited, Frome, Somerset
Colour origination by Positive Colour Limited, Essex
Produced in Portugal by Printer Portuguesa — Sintra

Bell & Hyman First Colour Dictionary has been designed for children who, having begun to read, are now ready for the first time for a genuine dictionary to help them.

In design and presentation this book is a real dictionary with definitions in alphabetical order. At the same time, since it is likely to be the child's first experience in using a reference book, the dictionary has been made as helpful and easy as possible, bearing in mind the child's present ability. For this reason, many of the conventions of the adult dictionary—unless they are meaningful for young children—have been avoided.

A child, starting to use a dictionary, needs to be able to find in it what a word means and how to spell it. This dictionary helps a child to achieve both these objectives. The meaning is conveyed by a definition, an illustrative sentence or a picture, used singly or together. The aim throughout is to make the meaning clear in whatever way is most appropriate. Only words defined elsewhere in this dictionary are used in defining other words.

Bell & Hyman First Colour Dictionary defines about 2,000 words. In addition, over 1,000 derived words, such as the irregular form of nouns and verbs, have been included to help both with spelling and vocabulary extension. In preparing this dictionary, use has been made of the vocabulary selection and definitions in *Boys' and Girls' First Dictionary* (now out of print) which I wrote with the late John Trevaskis. The words selected for inclusion are those most likely to be needed by children starting to use a dictionary. These words are based on the main reading schemes in use, on the considerable vocabulary research that has been carried out in recent years, and on advice from many educationists.

Simplicity and attractiveness are the main aims throughout, both to encourage the use of the dictionary and to ensure the child's understanding and enjoyment of it.

1985   Robin Hyman

A dictionary helps you to find out what words mean. It also shows you how to spell words. We hope you will enjoy using this dictionary.

When a word is printed with a star* next to it, this means that there is a picture of the word on the same page or the next page.

At the end of the book, you will find some useful lists of words:

about	1. to do with. This book is *about* words. 2. close to. My bedtime is *about* 8 o'clock.
above	over. The sky is *above* you.
abroad	in another country
absent	away; not present **absence**
accident*	Tom was hurt in an *accident*.
ache	a small pain that goes on and on **ached, aching, headache**
acorn	the nut of an oak tree
acrobat*	An *acrobat* does clever and daring tricks in a circus or theatre.
across	Ann walked *across* the road, from one side to the other.
act	take part in a play **acted, acting, actor, actress**
add	put together. If you *add* 2 and 2, it makes 4. **added, adding, addition**
address	the place where someone lives **addressed, addresses, addressing**
adult	a grown-up person
adventure	something exciting that happens **adventurous**
advertise	tell people that something is good to try to get them to buy it **advertisement, advertising**
aeroplane*	a machine that flies in the air
afraid	frightened. Mice are *afraid* of cats.
after	later; following. June is the month *after* May. **afterwards**
afternoon	the time between the middle of the day and the evening
again	once more; another time

accident

acrobat

aeroplane

A a

airport

alarm

album

against	1. Tom played tennis *against* Bob. 2. The ladder is *against* the wall.
age	how many years you have lived
ago	past. Tom came home an hour *ago*.
agree	think the same as someone else **agreed, agreeing**
air	Everyone breathes in *air*.
airport*	a place where aeroplanes take off and land **aircraft, aircrew**
alarm*	a warning sound. In the morning the *alarm* on the clock rings to wake you up. **fire-alarm, burglar-alarm**
album*	a book you put stamps or photos in
alike	looking or being almost the same
alive	living; not dead
alligator	a long, fierce animal. (See picture on page 8.)
allow	let somebody do something **allowed, allowing**
almost	nearly; not quite
alone	by yourself; on your own
along	Ann ran *along* the street.
alphabet	the 26 letters you use to make words: abcdefghijklmnopqrstuvwxyz **alphabetical order**
already	by now; before this time
also	as well
although	even if; though. *Although* it is raining, I will still go for a walk.
always	at all times; every time
amazing	surprising; very unusual
amber	a colour, like the middle colour of traffic lights. (See picture on page 26.)

ambulance*	a van that takes people who are ill or hurt to hospital
amount	how much you have
amuse	make somebody laugh **amused, amusement, amusing**
anchor*	a heavy hook that keeps a boat from moving about
angle	the space between 2 lines that meet
angry	very cross **anger, angrily**
animal*	Dogs, horses and lions are *animals*. (See picture on pages 8 and 9.)
ankle	the joint between your foot and your leg. (See picture on page 17.)
anorak*	a thick jacket with a hood and a zip
another	one more; a different one
answer	You *answer* if someone asks you a question. A sum has an *answer*. **answered, answering**
ant	a tiny insect that lives with thousands of others. (See picture on page 53.)
any	one of some. 'Have you *any* biscuits?' **anybody, anyone, anything, anywhere**
ape	a kind of monkey with no tail
apologise	say you are sorry
apple	a fruit with a core and pips. (See picture on page 43.)
April	the fourth month of the year
apron	what people wear to keep their clothes clean
are	There *are* 7 days in a week. **aren't = are not**
area	size; an amount of flat space covered by something

ambulance

anchor

anorak

A a   Animals

elephant

camel

rhinoceros

bear

hippopotamus

ox

reindeer

panda

horse

bull

tiger

pony

lion

cow

whale

giraffe

zebra

donkey

leopard

crocodile

deer

alligator

Animals

squirrel

tortoise

pig

mouse

hamster

gerbil

kangaroo

monkey

toad

rabbit

dog

guinea-pig

hare

lamb

bat

sheep

goat

hedgehog

fox

snail

rat

wolf

snake

cat

frog

arithmetic	sums; working with numbers
arm	the part of your body joined to your shoulder. (See picture on page 17.)
army	a large number of soldiers **armies**
around	on all sides
arrange	put things in order **arranged, arranging**
arrive	get to the end of a journey; reach **arrival, arrived, arriving**
arrow*	You shoot an *arrow* from a bow. An *arrow* shows you the way.
art	drawing and painting **artist**
ash	the dust left behind after something has burned **ashes**
ask	Teacher answers when I *ask* her a question. **asked, asking**
asleep	sleeping; not awake
assembly	You all come together for *assembly*.
astronaut*	someone who travels through space in a spaceship
ate	had some food (past of *eat*)
athletics	sports, like running and jumping **athlete**
atlas	a book of maps
August	the eighth month of the year
aunt	your mother's or father's sister; your uncle's wife **auntie, aunty**
autumn	the time of year between summer and winter
avenue*	a road with trees on both sides

arrow

astronaut

avenue

awake	not sleeping. Tom is wide *awake*.
away	not here; absent; not near
awful	very bad; terrible
axe*	a chopper with a long handle for cutting wood

axe

B b

baby	a very young boy or girl **babies**
back	the part behind; opposite of front **backwards**
bacon	meat from a pig
bad	not good; naughty
badge	You wear a *badge* to show you belong to a school or club.
bag	Ann carried the cakes home in a *bag*.
bake	cook food in an oven **baked, baking**
baker	a person who makes bread and cakes
ball	a round toy you play games and sports with
ballet	a kind of dancing in which the music and dance tell a story
balloon	a rubber bag you can blow up
banana	a long fruit with a yellow skin. (See picture on page 43.)
band*	1. people who play music together 2. You hold things together with an elastic or rubber *band*.
bandage*	a strip of cloth you tie over a cut
bang	a sudden, loud noise **banged, banging**

band 1

bandage

B b

bank	1. a building where people put money to keep it safe 2. the side of a river
bar	a long hard piece of something
barber	a person who cuts boys' and men's hair
bare	1. with nothing on; not covered ' 2. empty. The cupboard was *bare*.
bark	1. *Bark* covers the trunk of a tree. 2. the sound a dog makes **barked, barking**
barn	a shed where a farmer keeps his crops
barrow	a small cart with one wheel **wheelbarrow**
basin	a deep bowl or dish
basket*	a bag made of wood, straw or plastic
bat	1. a small animal which can fly. (See picture on page 9.) 2. You use a *bat* to play cricket.
bath	You wash yourself all over in a *bath*. **bathe, bathed, bathing, bathroom**
battery	You get electricity from a *battery*. **batteries**
battle	a fight in a war between groups of people
be	Tom wants to *be* in the concert. **been, being**
beach	the land at the edge of the sea **beaches**
bead	You thread *beads* on a string to make a necklace.
beak*	the hard part of a bird's mouth
bean	a seed; a green vegetable. (See picture on page 107.)
bear	a strong, hairy, wild animal. (See picture on page 8.)
beard*	hair that grows on a man's chin

basket

beak

beard

beat	1. win; do better than others 2. hit again and again; strike **beaten, beating**
beautiful	lovely; very pretty
because	why you do something
become	Ann hopes to *become* a doctor when she grows up. **became, becoming**
bed	You sleep in a *bed*. (See picture on page 51.) **bedroom, bedtime**
bee	an insect which makes honey. (See picture on page 53.) **beehive**
beef	meat from a cow or a bull
beer*	a kind of strong drink
beetle	a black insect. (See picture on page 53.)
before	sooner; earlier
beg	ask for something you want a lot **beggar, begged, begging**
begin	start **began, beginning, begun**
behave	do as you are told; be good **behaved, behaving, behaviour**
behind	at the back of something
believe	think that something is true **believed, believing**
bell*	A *bell* rings when you shake or press it.
belong	1. is owned by. This book *belongs* to me. 2. is a part of. Tom's brother *belongs* to the Scouts.
below	lower down; under
belt	a strap. Some people wear *belts*.
bench*	a long, wooden seat **benches**

beer

bell

bench

B b

bicycle

Birds

bend	curve; turn **bending, bent**
berry	a small juicy fruit **berries, blackberry, gooseberry, raspberry, strawberry**
best	finest; very good
better	1. Ann had a cold, but she is *better* now. 2. You work *better* when you try hard.
between	3 is the number *between* 2 and 4.
bicycle*	a machine with 2 wheels you can ride. **Bike** and **cycle** are short for *bicycle*.
big	large **bigger, biggest**
bill	1. A *bill* shows how much money you have to pay for something. 2. the beak of a bird
bin	a box to keep things in **bread-bin, dustbin**
bird*	All *birds* have wings, and most of them can fly.

budgerigar

canary

owl

robin

eagle

penguin

magpie

cuckoo

crow

pigeon parrot sparrow swallow thrush

birthday	the day of the year on which you were born
biscuit	a thin crisp cake
bit	a small piece
bite	cut with your teeth **bit, biting, bitten**
bitter	not sweet; with a nasty taste
black	a colour; very dark. (See picture on page 26.) **blackbird**
blackberry	a small black fruit that grows on a bush. (See picture on page 43.) **blackberries**
blackboard*	Teacher writes on the *blackboard* with chalk.
blame	tell someone you think what he or she has done is wrong **blamed, blaming**
blanket	a warm woollen cover on a bed. Ann has an extra *blanket* to keep warm in the winter.
blast-off	when a rocket is shot up into space
bleed	When you cut yourself, you *bleed*. **bled, bleeding**
blind	not able to see
blink	open and close your eyes quickly **blinked, blinking**
block	a big piece of wood, stone or metal
blood	the red liquid in your body
blossom*	flowers on a tree or bush
blot	a spot of ink **blotted, blotting**
blouse*	Girls often wear a *blouse* with a skirt.
blow	1. a hard hit; a hard knock 2. push air out of your mouth or nose. Use a handkerchief to *blow* your nose. **blew, blowing, blown**

blackboard

blossom

blouse

B b

bonfire

bonnet

boots 1

blue	a colour like the colour of the sky when it is sunny. (See picture on page 26.) **bluebell, blue-tit**
blunt	not sharp; not pointed
board	a long, wide piece of wood
boat	a small ship
body*	You wash your *body* in the bath. (See picture on page 17.)
boil	Water *boils* when it is so hot that it gives off steam. **boiled, boiling**
bolt	a piece of metal which holds things together
bone	a hard part of the body. Your skeleton is made of *bone*. **bony**
bonfire*	a fire in the open air
bonnet*	the part of a car that covers the engine
book	This *book* is called a dictionary. **bookcase, bookshelf, bookshop, notebook**
boot*	1. *Boots* cover your feet and ankles. 2. a place to put luggage at the back of a car
born	started life; began living
borrow	have something for a short time and then give it back **borrowed, borrowing**
both	two together
bottle	*Bottles* are made of glass or plastic and hold liquids.
bottom	the lowest part; underneath
bought	paid for something (past of *buy*)
bounce	spring up and down like a ball **bounced, bouncing**

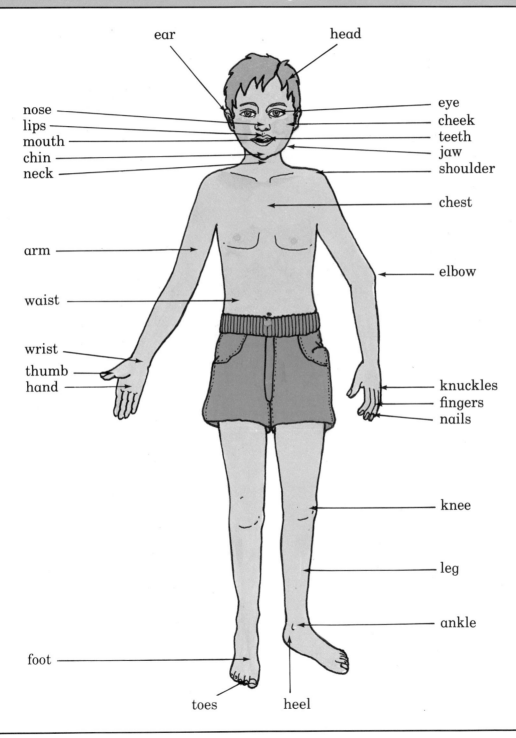

ear

head

nose

lips

mouth

chin

neck

eye

cheek

teeth

jaw

shoulder

chest

arm

elbow

waist

wrist

thumb

hand

knuckles

fingers

nails

knee

leg

ankle

foot

toes

heel

B b

bow	1. a kind of knot used for tying things 2. a bent piece of wood for shooting arrows 3. You play a violin with a *bow*.
bowl	a basin; a deep dish
box*	a case to keep things in. Teacher takes chalk from the *box*. **boxes, letter-box, pillar-box**
boy	a child; a young man. Tom is a *boy*.
bracelet*	a chain or band that you wear round your wrist
braces	1. wires a dentist puts on teeth to make them straight 2. Some men wear *braces* to hold up their trousers.
brake	You use *brakes* to stop or slow down a car or bicycle.
branch	part of a tree. A *branch* grows from the trunk. **branches**
brave	not afraid of danger
bread	a food made with flour
break	smash; split into pieces **breaking, broke, broken**
breakfast	the first meal of the day. Ann had *breakfast* before she went to school.
breath	air that goes in and out of your body **breathe, breathed, breathing**
brick	a block of hard clay. Houses are built with *bricks*.
bridge*	a path or road over a river or railway
bright	1. shining. The sun is *bright* in summer. 2. clever. Ann is a *bright* girl.
bring	fetch; carry **bringing, brought**
broke	smashed (past of *break*) **broken**

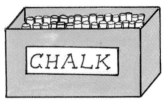

box

bracelet

bridge

brooch*	A girl sometimes pins a *brooch* on her dress. **brooches**
brook	a small stream
broom	a brush with a long handle
brother	a boy who has the same mother and father as you
brought	fetched (past of *bring*)
brown	a colour like chocolate. (See picture on page 26.)
Brownie	a junior Girl Guide
brush	You use a *brush* to paint with. **brushes**
bubble	a shiny ball that you make with soap and water
bucket*	a pail. You carry liquids in a *bucket*.
buckle	A *buckle* is used to fasten a belt or shoe.
bud	a leaf or flower before it opens. (See picture on page 41.)
budgerigar	a pet bird with bright colours; the short word for it is **budgie**. (See picture on page 14.)
build	make something. Men *build* houses. **builder, building, built**
bulb*	1. a fat part of some plants that grows in the ground 2. the glass part of an electric lamp
bull	a farm animal. (See picture on page 8.)
bump	a knock; a blow
bunch	a group of things, like a *bunch* of flowers **bunches**
bundle	many things tied together, like a *bundle* of sticks

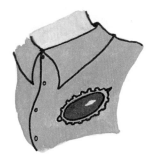

brooch

bucket

bulb 1

bungalow*	a house with no upstairs
burglar	A *burglar* breaks into houses to rob.
burn	be on fire **burned, burning, burnt**
burst	split open suddenly
bury	put into the ground and cover up **buried, buries, burying**
bus	a motor coach for carrying a lot of people **buses**
bush*	a small tree **bushes, bushy**
busy	having a lot to do **busier, busiest, business**
butcher	a person who sells meat
butter	*Butter* is made from milk. You spread *butter* on bread.
buttercup	a small yellow flower. (See picture on page 41.)
butterfly	an insect with pretty wings. (See picture on page 53.) **butterflies**
button	You use *buttons* to fasten clothes.
buy	get something by paying for it **bought, buyer, buying**

bungalow

bush

C c

cabbage	a green vegetable. (See picture on page 107.)
cabin	1. a wooden hut 2. a small room in a ship
café*	a place where you can buy a meal; a restaurant

café

cage	Animals are sometimes kept in *cages* at the zoo.
cake	a kind of sweet bread
calculator	a machine for doing hard sums quickly
calendar	a list of the days and months of the year
calf	a young cow **calves**
call	1. shout; cry out 2. name. My name is Thomas but they *call* me Tom. **called, calling**
came	arrived (past of *come*)
camel	an animal with a hump on its back. (See picture on page 8.)
camera*	You take pictures with a *camera*.
camp	a group of tents or caravans where people live
can	1. Tom *can* run fast if he tries. 2. a tin to keep things in **can't = can not**
canal	a river made by men for boats to use
canary	a small yellow bird. (See picture on page 14.) **canaries**
candle	A *candle* burns to give light.
canoe*	a small narrow boat
cap	1. Tom is wearing his new school *cap* on his head. 2. a lid; a cover
capital	a large letter in the alphabet, like A or B
captain	the leader of a team
car	Uncle took me for a ride in his *car*. **car-park**
caravan*	a small house on wheels

camera

cano

caravan

C c

cardigan

card	strong paper **cardboard, postcard**
cardigan*	a short woollen jacket with buttons
care	Take care when you cross the road. **careful, careless**
carol	a song you sing at Christmas
carpet	a big rug for covering the floor
carriage	the part of a train you travel in
carrot	an orange vegetable. (See picture on page 107.)
carry	pick up a thing and take it away **carried, carries, carrying**
cart	a wagon with wheels that is pulled by a horse
carve	1. cut meat into slices 2. cut wood or stone to make into a special shape **carved, carving**
case	a bag or box for carrying things
cassette*	a small case which holds tape for recording
castle	a big building with thick walls and towers
cat	a small pet animal covered with fur. (See picture on page 9.)
catch	get hold of **catches, catching, caught**
caterpillar	a grub that changes into a moth or butterfly. (See picture on page 53.)
cattle	cows and bulls
cauliflower	a green vegetable with a white top. (See picture on page 107.)
cave*	a large hole in a rock
ceiling	the roof of a room. (See picture on page 51.)

cassette

cave

celebrate	do something special because you are happy **celebrated, celebrating, celebration**
cent	a coin in some countries
centimetre	100 *centimetres* make 1 metre.
centre	the middle
certain	sure; knowing that something is true
chain*	rings joined together
chair	a seat with a back. (See picture on page 51.)
chalk	Teacher uses *chalk* to write on the blackboard.
change	1. the money you get back if you pay too much 2. put one thing in place of another; put on different clothes **changed, changing**
chapel*	a small church
chase	run after **chased, chasing**
cheap	not costing very much
cheat	win or get the right answer by breaking the rules
check	make sure that something is right
cheek	the side of your face. (See picture on page 17.)
cheerful	happy; jolly
cheese*	a food made from milk
chemist	A *chemist* sells medicine.
cherry	a small red fruit with a stone. (See picture on page 43.) **cherries**
chest	1. the front of the top of your body. (See picture on page 17.) 2. a big strong box

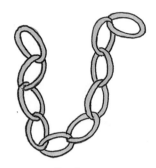

chain

chapel

cheese

C c

chicken	a young hen; a chick
child	a boy or girl **children**
chimney*	a hole in the roof to let smoke out
chin	the bottom of your face. (See picture on page 17.)
china	cups, saucers and plates
chip	a long piece of fried potato
chocolate	a sweet made from cocoa
choir*	a group of singers
choose	pick out one thing from many others **choosing, chose, chosen**
chop	1. a small piece of meat 2. cut something with an axe **chopped, chopper, chopping**
Christmas	December 25th; a festival to remember the birthday of Jesus.
church	a building where people go to pray **churches**
cinema	People go to see films in a *cinema*.
circle	a ring; a round shape
circus*	Animals and clowns do tricks in a *circus*. **circuses**
city	an important large town **cities**
clap	hit your hands together. We all *clapped* at the end of the pantomime. **clapped, clapping**
class	children who are taught together in school **classes, classroom**
clay	a soft, sticky kind of earth. You can make models or toys with *clay*.
clean	not dirty; not dusty **cleaner, cleanest**

chimney

choir

circus

clear	1. take or move something away 2. simple; easy to hear and understand 3. bright and sunny, with no clouds **cleared, clearing**
clever	able to do things well; bright
cliff*	steep rocks by the sea
climb	go up. Firemen *climb* ladders. **climbed, climbing**
cloakroom	You leave your coat in the *cloakroom* at school.
clock	A *clock* shows the time.
close	1. near; not far away 2. to shut **closed, closing**
cloth	material which is used to make clothes
clothes	the things you wear **clothing**
cloud	a grey or white shape in the sky that often brings rain **cloudy**
clown*	a funny man in a circus
club	1. a heavy wooden stick 2. People go to a *club* to meet their friends or play games.
clumsy	always knocking things over or dropping them
coach	a bus with one deck that you travel in for long journeys **coaches**
coal	*Coal* is put on a fire to make it burn.
coast	the land at the edge of the sea
coat*	You wear a *coat* over your other clothes. **overcoat, raincoat**
cobweb	a net made by a spider
cock	a kind of bird **cockerel**

cliff

clown

coat

C c

coconut

collar

cocoa	a chocolate drink
coconut*	a big nut with white juice inside
cod	a large fish
coffee	a drink. *Coffee* is made from the beans of a *coffee* bush.
coin	a piece of money
cold	1. not hot 2. an illness that makes you sneeze
collar*	A *collar* is worn round the neck.
collect	gathering things together. Some children *collect* stamps. **collected, collecting, collection**
colour*	1. Red, green and blue are *colours*. 2. to paint or crayon
comb	You can tidy your hair with a *comb*.
come	get to a place; reach **came, coming**

Colours

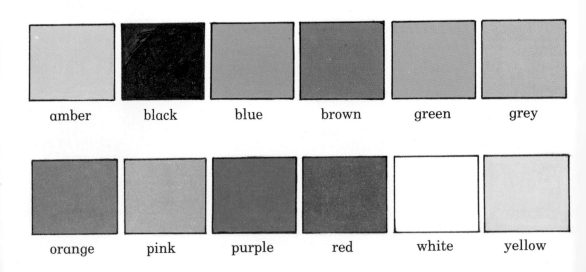

amber   black   blue   brown   green   grey

orange   pink   purple   red   white   yellow

C c

comic	a picture paper for children
common	1. often found; usual 2. land that anyone can use
compass	an instrument which shows the way. A *compass* has a needle which points to the north.
computer*	a machine that can do the work of many calculators at the same time
concert	music played for people to listen to
concrete	a kind of stone that builders make
conductor	1. A *conductor* takes the fares on a bus. 2. a person who guides an orchestra or band
conjurer*	A *conjurer* does clever tricks.
contain	hold something inside **contained, container, containing**
cook	to get food ready by heating it **cooked, cooker, cooking**
cool	not very hot; fairly cold
copy	do the same as everyone else **copied, copies, copying**
cord	very strong string
core	There is a *core* inside an apple.
cork	a stopper for a bottle
corn	a plant like wheat **corn-field, cornflake**
corner	the place where two walls or roads meet
correct	right; with no mistakes
corridor	a narrow passage in a building
cost	how much you pay for something; price
costume	1. dress 2. clothes you wear in a play
cot	a baby's bed
cottage*	a small house

computer

conjurer

cottage

C c

cowboy

cotton	1. a thin thread used for sewing 2. a kind of cloth
cough	a noise coming from your throat. The dust in the air made Anne *cough*.
could	past of *can* **couldn't**
count	add up; find out how many there are **counted, counting**
counter	1. a table in a shop 2. You sometimes use *counters* in playing games and doing sums.
country	1. a land. England is a *country*. 2. not in the town **countries**
couple	two (2); a pair
course	Of *course* Ann likes ice-cream.
cousin	a child of your aunt or uncle
cover	put one thing over another; hide something **covered, covering**
cow	a farm animal that gives us milk. (See picture on page 8.)
cowboy*	A *cowboy* rides a horse and looks after cattle.
crab*	a small sea animal with a shell
crack	split; break open. The snail lived in a *crack* in the wall. **cracked, cracking**
cracker	1. a toy you pull to make a bang 2. a kind of biscuit
cradle	a baby's cot that rocks
crane*	a machine that lifts and moves heavy things
crash	a loud noise when anything breaks; an accident **crashed, crashes, crashing**

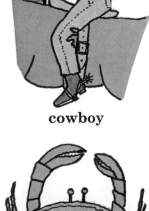

crab

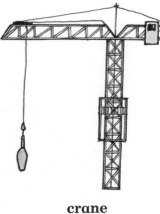

crane

crawl	move slowly along on your hands and knees; creep **crawled, crawling**
crayon	a stick of chalk used to colour pictures
cream	a thick, sweet kind of milk
creature	a person or an animal
creep	move along very quietly and slowly **creeping, crept**
crew	the people who work on a ship or aircraft
cricket*	1. a game played in summer 2. an insect that jumps. (See picture on page 53.)
cried	was in tears (past of *cry*)
crisp	1. hard and thin, but easy to break 2. a thin piece of fried potato
crocodile	a fierce animal that lives in rivers. (See picture on page 8.)
crocus	a small purple or yellow flower that grows in spring. (See picture on page 41.) **crocuses**
crooked	bent or twisted
crops	the plants a farmer grows
cross	1. a mark like this: X 2. angry; not pleased 3. Take care when you *cross* the road. **crossed, crosses, crossing**
crow	a black bird. (See picture on page 14.)
crowd*	a large number of people
crown*	A king or queen wears a *crown*.
cruel	hurting people; very unkind
crumb	a tiny bit of bread or cake
crust	the hard outside part of a loaf or pie
cry	1. let tears fall from your eyes 2. shout; speak very loudly **cried, cries, crying**

cricket 1

crowd

crown

Cc/Dd

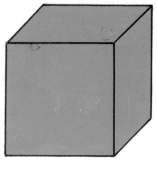

cube

cub	1. Some baby animals are called *cubs*. 2. a junior Scout
cube*	a shape that has 6 square sides
cuckoo	a bird that gets its name from the sound it makes. (See picture on page 14.)
cup	You drink tea or coffee out of a *cup*.
cupboard	A *cupboard* has shelves and you keep things in it. (See picture on page 51.)
curl	hair twisted into the shape of a ring **curly**
currant	a small fruit often put in cakes
curry	a tasty hot sauce to put on meat, eggs or vegetables
curtain*	cloth hung over windows. (See picture on page 51.)
curve	a bend; a part of a circle **curved, curving**
cushion*	a soft pillow used on a seat
custard	a sweet yellow sauce on a pudding
customer	someone who buys things
cut	use a knife or scissors **cutting**
cycle	ride a bicycle **cyclist**

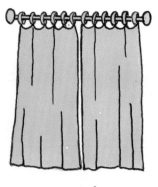

curtain

Dd

daddy	a child's name for father
daffodil	a yellow spring flower. (See picture on page 41.)
daily	each day
dairy	You get milk and butter at a *dairy*. **dairies**

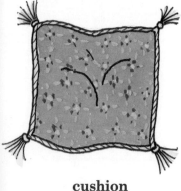

cushion

D d

daisy	a small white flower. (See picture on page 41.) **daisies**
damp	a bit wet
dance*	move in time to music **danced, dancer, dancing**
dandelion	a bright yellow wild flower. (See picture on page 41.)
dangerous	not safe **danger**
dare	try to make someone do something he ought not to do **dared, daring**
dark	without light; black **darker, darkest, darkness**
dart*	A *dart* has a sharp point and you throw it at a board.
date*	1. the time when something happens 2. a sweet, brown fruit
daughter	a girl child
dawn	first thing in the morning. It starts to get light at *dawn*.
day	1. 24 hours make 1 *day*. 2. the time when it is light **daily, daylight, daytime**
dead	not living; not alive
dear	1. costing a lot of money 2. loved; very much liked by you
December	the last month of the year
decide	make up your mind **decided, deciding**
deck	a floor on a ship or bus
deep	a long way down
deer	an animal that runs fast. (See picture on page 8.)

dance

dart

TUESDAY
10
AUGUST

date 1

D d

dentist

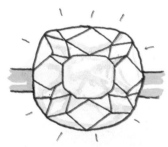

diamond

dinosaur

delighted	very pleased; happy **delight, delightful**
den	Some wild animals live in *dens*.
dentist*	A *dentist* takes care of your teeth.
desk	a table where you read and write
dew	drops of water on the ground early in the morning
diamond*	a bright jewel which costs a lot
dice	a cube which has numbers or spots on its 6 sides
dictionary	a book telling you what words mean
did	Yesterday we *did* sums. (past of *do*) **didn't = did not**
die	stop living. Ann will be sad if her pet rabbits *die*. **died, dies, dying**
different	not the same; not like **difference**
difficult	hard to do
dig	use a spade to move soil **digging, dug**
digital	A *digital* watch shows the time in numbers.
dinner	the main meal of the day **dine, dining-room**
dinosaur*	a very large animal that lived millions of years ago
dirty	not clean; needing a wash
disappear	vanish; go away without anybody knowing where
disappointed	sad because what you wanted has not happened
disc	a record
disease	an illness

dish	a kind of plate **dishes**
dislike	not liking somebody or something
ditch	a long hole by the side of a road for carrying water away **ditches**
dive	jump head first into deep water **dived, diving**
divide	share; split something into parts **divided, dividing, division**
do	We *do* sums at school. **did, didn't, does, doesn't, doing, done, don't**
dock*	a place where ships are loaded
doctor	A *doctor* helps to make you better when you are ill.
dog	an animal which barks. (See picture on page 9.)
doll	a toy model of a person
dollar	a sum of money in some countries
dominoes*	a game. *Dominoes* are pieces of wood with spots on one side.
donkey	an animal with large ears. (See picture on page 8.)
door	the way into a room or house. (See picture on page 51.)
double	twice as big; twice as much
down	in or to a lower place **downhill, downstairs.** (See picture on page 51.)
dozen	12; twelve
drag	pull something heavy along **dragged, dragging**
dragon*	a fierce make-believe animal. You read about *dragons* in fairy tales.

dock

dominoes

dragon

D d

drain	a pipe where water runs away
draw	1. make a picture 2. when two teams score the same in a match **drawing, drawn, drew**
drawer	a sliding box in a table or chest
dream	what you see or think in your sleep **dreamed, dreaming, dreamt**
dress	1. put clothes on 2. A girl wears a *dress*. **dressed, dresses, dressing**
drink	swallow something like water. You *drink* when you are thirsty. **drank, drinking, drunk**
drip	fall in drops **dripped, dripping**
drive	1. make a car go 2. a path which leads to a house **driven, driver, driving, drove**
drop	1. a small wet spot 2. let something fall **dropped, dropping**
drown	die under water **drowned, drowning**
drum*	You beat a *drum* with sticks.
dry	not wet. She washed the clothes and hung them up to *dry*. **dried, drier, dries, driest, drying**
duck*	a bird which swims
dull	not bright. The grey clouds made the day very *dull*.
dusk	the end of the day when it begins to get dark
dust	tiny bits of dry earth; dirt **dustbin, dustman**
dwarf*	someone much smaller than others **dwarves**

drum

duck

dwarf

each	every one
eagle	a large fierce bird. (See picture on page 14.)
ear	You hear with your *ears*. (See picture on page 17.)
early	not late; in time
earn	to be paid for work you do **earned, earning**
earth	1. the world 2. the soil; the ground
easel*	a stand to hold up a painting or a blackboard
east*	1. a point on the compass 2. where the sun rises
Easter	a festival in spring
easy	simple; not difficult **easier, easiest, easily**
eat	put food in your mouth to swallow **ate, eaten, eating**
edge	the top, bottom or side of something
egg*	Birds lay *eggs*.
eight	the number 8 **eighth (8th), eighteen (18), eighty (80)**
either	one out of two different things. Tom is coming *either* today or tomorrow.
elastic	a strip of rubber which stretches
elbow	the joint in the middle of your arm. (See picture on page 17.)
electricity	You switch on *electricity* to give light or heat. **electric, electrical, electrician**
elephant	a very large animal with a trunk. (See picture on page 8.)
eleven	the number 11 **eleventh (11th)**

easel

east 1

eggs

E e

emerald

envelope

escalator

elf	a kind of fairy in a story **elves**
elm	a tall tree
else	other than. Has anybody *else* except Tom got a cold?
emerald*	a bright green jewel
empty	with nothing in it
end	stop; finish **ended, ending**
enemy	someone who hates you and wants to hurt you
engine	a machine for doing work. An *engine* drives a car.
enjoy	to like doing something **enjoyed, enjoying**
enormous	very big; huge
enough	as much as you need or want
enter	go into **entered, entering, entrance**
envelope*	You send a letter in an *envelope*.
equal	the same. 2 threes are *equal* to six.
escalator*	a moving staircase to take you up or down
escape	get away from something; get out **escaped, escaping**
even	1. flat and smooth; not rough 2. 4, 6 and 8 are *even* numbers.
evening	the time before it gets dark
ever	always; at any time
every	all; each one **everybody, everyone, everything, everywhere**
excellent	very good; the best
except	leaving out. We were all at school *except* Tom, who was ill.

exciting	full of adventure; lively
excuse	the reason you give for something naughty you have done
exercise	1. to practise often 2. using your muscles
exit	the way out
expect	think something will happen soon **expected, expecting**
explain	say what something means **explained, explaining**
explode	go off with a bang; blow up **exploded, exploding, explosion**
explore	go to find out about a new place **explored, explorer*, exploring**
express*	a fast train or coach; a fast service
extra	more than usual; more than enough
eye	You see with your *eyes*. (See picture on page 17.) **eyebrow, eyelid, eyesight**

explorer

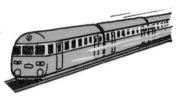

express

F f

face	the front of your head
fact	something that is true
factory	a building where things are made **factories**
fail	try to do something and not be able to do it **failed, failing, failure**
fair*	1. not dark; light. Ann has *fair* hair and blue eyes. 2. right; just 3. a place for fun where there are roundabouts and stalls

fair 3

F f

farm

feather

fence

fairy	a small make-believe person who does magic in stories **fairies**
fall	drop. Apples *fall* off trees. **fallen, falling, fell**
family	a mother and father and their children **families**
famous	very well known
far	a long way off **farther, farthest**
fare	You pay a *fare* on a bus or train.
farm*	A farmer keeps animals and grows crops on a *farm*. **farmer, farmhouse, farmyard**
fast	quick; going at great speed **faster, fastest**
fasten	tie; fix firmly **fastened, fastening**
fat	1. big; round; not thin 2. the greasy part of meat **fatter, fattest**
father	a man who has children; daddy
favourite	the one you like best
feather*	*Feathers* grow on birds.
February	the second month of the year
feed	give food to. Ann *feeds* the cat. **fed, feeding**
feel	1. touch 2. Tom *feels* cold in icy weather. **feeling, felt**
feet	more than one *foot*. I have 2 *feet*. (See picture on page 17.)
fence*	a wall made of wood or wire round a garden or field
festival	a time when you celebrate something special

fetch	go and get **fetched, fetches, fetching**
few	a small number; not many
field	a piece of land on a farm
fierce	wild, like a tiger
fifteen	the number 15 **fifteenth (15th)**
fifty	the number 50
fight	The two boys had a *fight* and hit each other. **fighting, fought**
figure	a number. 2 and 3 are *figures*.
fill	put in so much that there is no room for any more. Please *fill* the kettle. **filled, filling**
film	1. a moving picture you see in a cinema or on television 2. You put a *film* in a camera so that you can take photographs.
fin	A fish uses its *fins* to swim.
find	see something you are looking for **finding, found**
fine	1. sunny; when the weather is good 2. very good; excellent
finger	a part of your hand. (See picture on page 17.) **finger-nail, finger-print**
finish	end; stop **finished, finishes, finishing**
fir*	a tree. Small *fir* trees are used as Christmas trees.
fire	1. something burning 2. shoot with a gun **fire-engine*, fireman, fireplace, fire-station, bonfire**
firework*	Rockets and crackers are *fireworks*.

fir

fire-engine

fireworks

F f

first	1st; before anyone or anything else
fish	A *fish* lives in water. A herring is a *fish*. **fishes, goldfish**
fist*	a hand closed tightly
fit	1. healthy; well and strong 2. to be the right size **fitted, fitting**
five	the number 5 **fifth (5th), fifteen (15), fifty (50)**
fix	fasten; stick things together **fixed, fixes, fixing**
flag*	a coloured piece of cloth on a pole
flake	a small, thin piece, like a snow*flake* or corn*flake*
flame*	the shining part when a fire burns brightly
flap	move up and down like wings **flapped, flapping**
flash	a sudden bright light **flashed, flashes, flashing**
flat	1. smooth; without lumps 2. a set of rooms for living in
floor	the part of a room you walk on
flour	Bread and cakes are made with *flour*.
flower*	a blossom; the bright part of a plant. (See picture on page 41.)
fly	1. a small insect. (See picture on page 53.) 2. move through the air **flew, flies, flight, flying**
foggy	when the air is thick and you cannot see very far
fold	bend something over **folded, folding**
follow	go or come after. May *follows* April. **followed, following**

fist

flag

flame

40

Flowers

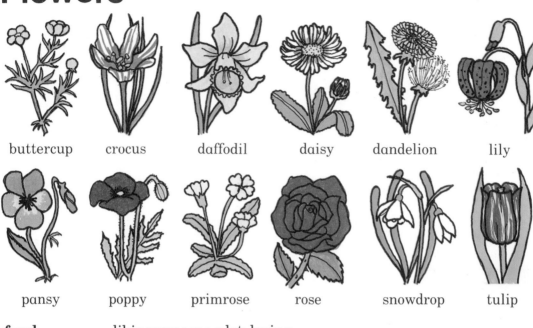

buttercup	crocus	daffodil	daisy	dandelion	lily
pansy	poppy	primrose	rose	snowdrop	tulip

fond	liking someone a lot; loving
food	*Food* is what you eat.
foot	1. the part at the end of your leg. (See picture on page 17.) 2. an old measure. 1 *foot* is equal to about $\frac{1}{3}$ of a metre. **feet, football, footpath, footstep**
forest	a big wood; a lot of trees together
forget	not able to remember **forgetting, forgot, forgotten**
fork	You pick up food with a *fork*.
fortnight	2 weeks; 14 days
forty	the number 40
forward	to the front
fought	had a fight (past of *fight*)
found	I *found* the hat which I had lost. (past of *find*)

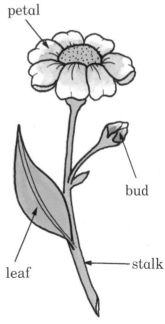

petal

bud

leaf

stalk

F f

fountain*	water shooting into the air
four	the number 4 **fourth (4th), fourteen (14), forty (40)**
fox	a wild animal like a fierce dog. (See picture on page 9.) **foxes**
fraction	a part of all of something, like a half ($\frac{1}{2}$) or a third ($\frac{1}{3}$) or a quarter ($\frac{1}{4}$)
frame*	the wood or metal part round a picture
free	not costing anything
freeze	make very cold. Water *freezes* to ice. **freezer, freezing, froze, frozen**
fresh	new; just made or picked
Friday	the sixth day of the week
fridge	short word for **refrigerator**
friend	someone you know well and like
frightened	afraid; when you are scared. The loud bang *frightened* me.
frog	a small jumping animal that lives near water. (See picture on page 9.)
front	the first part; opposite of back. The visitor came to the *front* door.
frost	thin white ice that covers the ground in cold weather **frosty**
fruit*	Apples and pears are *fruit*. (See picture on page 43.)
fry	cook food in hot fat **fried, fries, frying**
full	when there is no room for any more
funny	making you laugh; very amusing
fur	the soft hair on some animals
furniture*	things in your house, like chairs and tables

fountain

frame

furniture

Fruit

apple

banana

blackberry

gooseberry

grapefruit

cherry

pear

lemon

grapes

melon

strawberry

orange

plum

raspberry

peach

G g

gale	a very strong wind
gallon	a measure of liquids like petrol equal to about 4½ litres; 1 *gallon* = 8 pints
gallop	run fast like a horse **galloped, galloping**
game	sport; something you play, like football
gang	a group of people doing things together
garage*	a building where a car is kept or mended
garden	the ground near a house used for growing flowers or vegetables
gas	something like air. When *gas* burns, it gives light and heat. **gases**

garage

G g

giant

globe

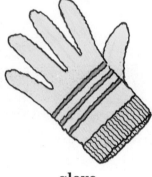

glove

gate	a door in a fence or wall
gather	collect; pick up things and put them together **gathered, gathering**
gave	Ann *gave* me a sweet. (past of *give*)
gentle	quiet and kind
geography	You learn about countries and places in *geography*.
gerbil	a small furry animal with a long tail often kept as a pet. (See picture on page 9.)
get	1. I always *get* to school early. 2. bring. Go and *get* the book. **getting, got**
giant*	1. a big ugly man in fairy tales 2. very big; huge
giraffe	an animal with a very long neck. (See picture on page 8.)
girl	a child; a young woman. Ann is a *girl*.
give	hand something to someone **gave, gift, given, giving**
glad	pleased; cheerful
glass	Windows are made of *glass*.
glasses	People wear *glasses* to see better.
globe*	a large ball with a map of the world on it
glove*	You wear *gloves* on your hands.
glue	a liquid that sticks things together
go	move; leave **goes, going, gone, went**
goal	You try to kick the ball into *goal* at football. **goal-keeper, goal-post**
goat	a small animal with horns. (See picture on page 9.)

gold — a bright metal that costs a lot
golden

goldfish* — a pet fish with bright colours
goldfishes

golf — an outdoor game played with a small white ball

good — nice; kind; pleasing
goodbye, goodnight

goose* — a bird like a large duck
geese

gooseberry — a small green fruit. (See picture on page 43.)
gooseberries

gorilla — a very large ape

grab — catch hold of something; snatch
grabbed, grabbing

grain* — seed of corn or wheat

gram — a small weight or measure. 1,000 *grams* make 1 kilogram.

grand — great; fine

grandfather — the father of your mother or father
grand-dad, grandpa

grandmother — the mother of your father or mother
grandma, granny

grape — a small black or green fruit. *Grapes* grow in bunches. (See picture on page 43.)

grapefruit — a yellow fruit, like a big orange. (See picture on page 43.)

grass — a green plant that grows to make a lawn
grasshopper

gravy — a thick sauce made from the juice of meat

grease — thick oil or melted fat
greasy

great — very large; important
greater, greatest

goldfish

goose

grain

G g

greedy	eating too much; selfish
green	a colour like grass. (See picture on page 26.)
greengrocer	A *greengrocer* sells fruit and vegetables.
greenhouse*	a glass building where plants grow
grey	a colour like an elephant. (See picture on page 26.)
grip	hold something very tight **gripped, gripping**
grocer	A *grocer* sells food like sugar and biscuits. **grocery, groceries**
ground	earth; soil; land
group	a number of people or things
grow	1. get bigger 2. plant seeds in the ground and look after them **grew, growing, grown, grown-up**
grub	a tiny young insect
grunt	the noise made by a pig
guard*	1. A *guard* waves a flag for the driver to start a train. 2. keep safe; look after **guarded, guarding**
guess	say what you think is right although you are not sure **guessed, guesses, guessing**
guide	show someone the way; lead **guided, guiding**
guinea-pig	a small furry animal with no tail often kept as a pet. (See picture on page 9.)
guitar*	a musical instrument
gum	1. a sweet which you chew 2. You use *gum* to stick things together. 3. Your teeth grow from your *gums*.

greenhouse

guard 1

guitar

gun	A *gun* is used to shoot with.
gutter	the edge of a road where the water runs away

hamburger

H h

had	Tom *had* a cold. (past of *have*) **hadn't = had not**
hair	*Hair* grows on your head. **hairdresser, hairy**
half	½; what you get when you divide something into 2 equal parts **halves**
hall	1. the passage inside the front door 2. a large room where people meet
ham	meat from a pig
hamburger*	a round flat piece of minced beef which is often eaten in a bread roll
hammer*	You use a *hammer* to knock nails in.
hamster	a small furry animal with a short tail, often kept as a pet. (See picture on page 9.)
hand	the part at the end of your arm. (See picture on page 17.) **handbag*, handful**
handkerchief	a small piece of cloth or paper tissue you use to wipe your nose
handle	the part of a thing that you hold **handlebars**
hang	put something up on a hook **hanging, hung**
happen	take place. A very funny thing *happened* yesterday. **happened, happening**
happy	cheerful; glad; pleased **happier, happiest, happily, happiness**

hammer

handbag

H h

hat

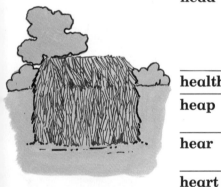

haystack

heater

hard	1. difficult 2. not soft **harder, hardest, hardly**
hare	an animal like a large rabbit. (See picture on page 9.)
harvest	the crops that a farmer gathers when they are ripe
hat*	You wear a *hat* on your head.
hate	dislike someone a lot **hated, hating**
have	hold; own. I *have* a new bicycle. **had, hadn't, has, hasn't, haven't, having**
hay	dried grass. Horses and cows eat *hay*. **haystack***
head	1. your body above the neck. (See picture on page 17.) 2. the most important **headache, headmaster, headmistress, head-teacher**
healthy	fit; feeling well; not ill
heap	a pile; many things lying on top of each other
hear	listen to. We *hear* sounds with our ears. **heard, hearing**
heart	the part of you that sends blood round your body
heat	A fire gives out *heat* to make you warm. **heated, heater*, heating**
heavy	not easy to lift; weighing a lot **heavier, heaviest, heavily**
hedge	a fence of bushes
hedgehog	a small wild animal with prickles. (See picture on page 9.)
heel	the back of your foot. (See picture on page 17.)
height	how high something is

H h

helicopter*	a kind of small aeroplane that can take off and land without a runway
help	do something for someone **helped, helping**
hen	a bird that lays eggs that you eat
here	in this place; present
herring	a fish
herself	Ann comes to school by *herself*.
hide	1. put a thing where it cannot be seen 2. go where no one can find you **hid, hidden, hiding**
high	tall; far up; above other things **higher, highest**
hill	a small mountain
himself	Tom fell over and hurt *himself*.
hip	the joint between your leg and your body
hippopotamus	a very large animal that lives in a river. Hippo is short for *hippopotamus*. (See picture on page 8.)
history	You learn in *history* about things that happened in the past.
hit	strike; give someone a blow; tap **hitting**
hive*	Bees live in a bee*hive*.
hobby	something you enjoy doing in your spare time like collecting stamps **hobbies**
hold	1. have something in your hands 2. have room for **held, holder, holding**
hole	a space; an opening in something
holiday	You do not work on *holiday*.
holly*	a bush with prickles and red berries
home	the place where you live

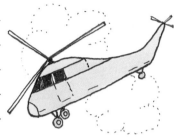

helicopter

hive

holly

H h

honey	a sweet juice made by bees
hood*	a soft cover for your head and neck
hoof	the hard part of the foot of an animal like a horse **hooves**
hook	a bent piece of metal for hanging things on
hop	jump up and down on one foot **hopped, hopping**
hope	wish that something pleasant will happen **hoped, hoping**
horn	a sharp pointed bone on the head of some animals
horrible	shocking; awful
horrid	nasty
horse	a large animal. Ann rides a *horse*. (See picture on page 8.)
hose*	a long rubber or plastic pipe
hospital	a place where people who are ill are looked after
hot	very warm **hotter, hottest**
hotel	a place where people pay to stay
hour	60 minutes make 1 *hour*. 24 *hours* make 1 day.
house*	a building for living in. (See picture on page 51.)
hug	hold tightly in your arms **hugged, hugging**
huge	very large; enormous
hump*	a large lump on an animal's back
hundred	the number 100
hungry	needing food
hunt	look for something; search **hunted, hunting**

hood

hose

hump

House

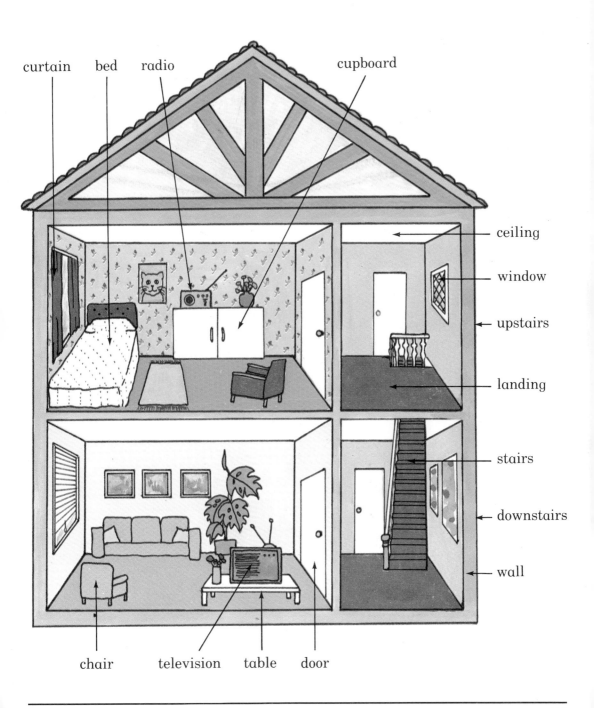

curtain bed radio cupboard

ceiling

window

upstairs

landing

stairs

downstairs

wall

chair television table door

hutch

hurry	go or move quickly; rush **hurried, hurries, hurrying**
hurt	give someone pain **hurting**
husband	a man who is married
hut	a small building made of wood
hutch*	a cage for keeping rabbits **hutches**
hymn	You sing *hymns* at prayers or in church.

I i

icicles

ice	very cold water that has turned hard **ice-cream, icicle*, icy, iceberg**
icing	a sweet covering on cakes
idle	doing nothing; lazy
ill*	not feeling well; sick **illness**
important	great; large
inch	an old measure. 1 *inch* is equal to about $2\frac{1}{2}$ centimetres. **inches**
indoors	inside a building
infant	a baby; a very young child
ink	You use *ink* in a pen for writing.
insect*	a tiny creature with 6 legs. (See picture on page 53.)
inside	in
instead	in place of
instrument	1. something you play to make music 2. a tool used to make or show something
interesting	makes you want to know more

ill

Insects

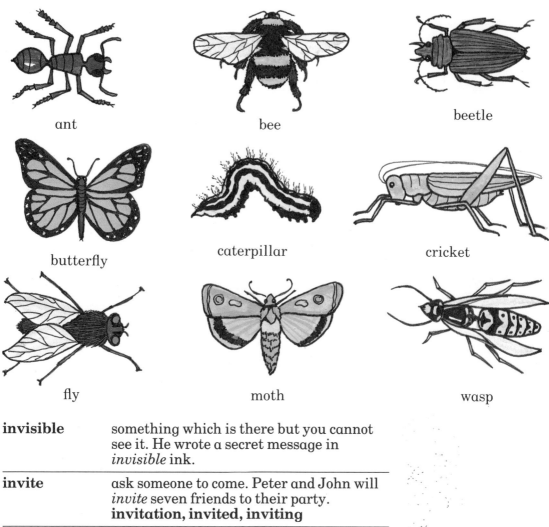

ant

bee

beetle

butterfly

caterpillar

cricket

fly

moth

wasp

invisible	something which is there but you cannot see it. He wrote a secret message in *invisible* ink.
invite	ask someone to come. Peter and John will *invite* seven friends to their party. **invitation, invited, inviting**
iron*	1. An *iron* is used to press clothes flat after they have been washed. 2. a hard metal
is	Grass *is* green. **isn't = is not**
island	land with water all round it
ivy	a plant that grows up walls

iron 1

J j

jam

jacket	a short coat
jam*	a sweet food made with fruit
January	the first month of the year
jar	A *jar* is made of glass or plastic and holds things like jam.
jaw	the bones round a mouth. (See picture on page 17.)
jeans	trousers made of heavy blue cloth
jelly	a shiny food made with fruit juices **jellies**
jersey	a shirt you wear when you play games like football
jet	a very fast plane
jewel	a pretty stone that costs a lot **jewellery**
jigsaw*	a picture cut up into pieces that you fit together
job	a piece of work
join	1. Tom and Ann *join* in the singing. 2. fix together; fasten **joined, joining**
joint	1. a piece of meat 2. the place where two parts join
joke	a very funny short story
jolly	merry; full of fun; happy
journey	when you travel to a place; a trip
joy	great happiness
jug	You keep liquids like milk in a *jug*.
juice	the liquid from fruit or meat **juicy**
July	the seventh month of the year
jump	spring up and down **jumped, jumping**
jumper*	a blouse made of wool

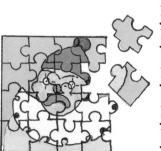

jigsaw

jumper

junction	a place where two or more roads meet
June	the sixth month of the year
jungle	a thick wild forest in a hot country
junior	younger
just	1. not long ago 2. fair; right

kennel

K k

kangaroo	an animal with long back legs on which it jumps along. (See picture on page 9.)
keep	1. have; look after 2. go on doing something 3. stay fresh; not go bad **keeper, keeping, kept**
kennel*	a small hut for a dog
kerb	the edge of the pavement
kettle*	You boil water in a *kettle*.
key	You use a *key* to undo a lock. **keyhole**
kick	hit with your foot **kicked, kicking**
kid	a young goat
kill	make someone die **killed, killing**
kilogram	1,000 grams make 1 *kilogram*.
kilometre	1,000 metres make 1 *kilometre*.
kilt*	a coloured skirt. Some men in Scotland wear *kilts*.
kind	1. friendly; good to others 2. a sort
king	a man who is the head of a country **kingdom**

kettle

kilt

K k / L l

kite

kiss	touch with your lips **kissed, kisses, kissing**
kitchen	the room where food is cooked
kite*	a toy that you can fly
kitten	a young cat
knee	the joint in the middle of your leg. (See picture on page 17.)
kneel	go down on your knees **kneeling, knelt**
knew	Tom *knew* the letters before he started school. (past of *know*)
knickers	pants; clothes a girl wears next to her skin on the lower part of her body
knife	You use a *knife* to cut with. **knives, penknife**
knit	make clothes with needles and wool **knitted, knitting**
knob*	a door handle
knock	hit or tap something. *Knock* at the door before you go in. **knocked, knocking**
knot*	the place where string or rope is tied
know	I *know* my letters, because I have just learned them. **knew, knowing, knowledge, known**
knuckle	a joint in your finger. (See picture on page 17.)

knob

knot

L l

label	My pencil-case has a *label* on to show it belongs to me.
lace	a kind of string. Some shoes are tied with *laces*.

ladder*	a set of steps for climbing
lady	a polite name for a woman **ladies**
lake	water with land round it
lamb	a young sheep. (See picture on page 9.)
lamp	a light covered by glass **lamp post, lampshade**
land	earth; the ground
landing	1. the space at the top of the stairs. (See picture on page 51.) 2. coming down to the ground, as a plane does
lane	1. a narrow road in the country 2. a part of the road for one line of traffic
lantern*	a lamp that you can carry
larder	a cupboard where food is kept
large	big; great **larger, largest**
last	1. at the end. The *last* letter of the alphabet is Z. 2. go on for a long time. Suck your sweet to make it *last*.
late	not early; after the right time **lately, later, latest**
laugh	the sound you make when you think something is funny **laughed, laughing, laughter**
launch	1. a large motor-boat 2. send a rocket into space **launched, launching**
laundry	a place where clothes are washed **laundries, launderette***
lavatory	a toilet; a W.C. **lavatories**
lawn	grass which is cut short

ladder

lantern

launderette

leaves

leap

leather

lay	1. Hens *lay* eggs. 2. arrange things, like cups and saucers, on a table 3. rested (past of *lie*) **laid, laying**
lazy	idle; not wanting to work
lead	1. a heavy grey metal 2. be at the front **leader, leading, led**
leaf	part of a plant or tree **leaves***
lean	1. thin 2. bend towards; rest against **leaned, leaning, leant**
leap*	a big jump
leap year	a year every 4 years when February has 29 days instead of 28 days. 1984 and 1988 are leap years.
learn	get to know. We *learn* how to write at school. **learned, learning, learnt**
least	the smallest amount
leather*	Shoes and handbags are often made of *leather*.
leave	1. go away 2. put something down **leaving, left**
left	opposite of right
leg	a part of your body you walk with. (See picture on page 17.)
lemon	a yellow fruit with a sour taste. (See picture on page 43.) **lemonade**
lend	let someone use something of yours and then give it back to you **lending, lent**
length	how long something is

leopard	a fierce animal with a spotted skin. (See picture on page 8.)
less	a smaller number; not as much
lesson	the time in school you spend doing one thing, like sums
let	allow **letting**
letter	1. a message you write and send to someone 2. a part of the alphabet, like A, B or C **letter-box**
lettuce	a vegetable with green leaves. (See picture on page 107.)
library*	a room or building where books are kept **libraries, librarian**
lick	touch with your tongue **licked, licking**
lid	a cover; a top
lie	1. say something which is not true 2. rest. Ann had a headache so she went to *lie* down. **lay, lied, lies, lying**
life	the time when we are alive **lives, lifeboat**
lift	1. pick up 2. a kind of cage for carrying you up or down in a building **lifted, lifting**
light	1. bright; not dark 2. not heavy 3. set fire to something **lighter, lightest, lighthouse*, lighting, lightning, lit, daylight**
like	1. be fond of 2. almost the same; not much different **liked, liking**
lilac*	a bush with white or mauve flowers

library

lighthouse

lilac

L l

loaves

lily	a large white flower. (See picture on page 41.) **lilies**
line	1. a long narrow mark 2. a row of things or people 3. a piece of rope or string
lion	a strong, wild animal. (See picture on page 8.)
lip	the edge of your mouth. (See picture on page 17.)
liquid	something which is wet, like water
list	things written one after the other
listen	hear sounds; try to hear **listened, listening**
lit	set fire to (past of *light*)
litre	a measure for liquids
little	small; not much
live	1. have a home. Tom *lives* in a house. 2. be alive **lived, lively, living**
load	things to be carried or moved
loaf	A *loaf* of bread can be sliced or unsliced, brown or white. **loaves***
lock*	fasten a door with a key **locked, locking**
log	a large piece of wood cut from a tree
lonely	by yourself; having no friends
long	not short; measuring a lot
look	watch; see **looked, looking**
loose	not fastened or tight; able to move about
lord	master or ruler
lorry*	a large motor for carrying loads **lorries**

lock

lorry

lose	1. not to be able to find something 2. not to win; to be beaten **losing, lost**
lot	a large number; many
loud	noisy; easy to hear **louder, loudest, loudly**
love	be very fond of **loved, loving**
lovely	beautiful; pretty
low	not high or tall **lower, lowest**
lucky	Tom was *lucky* to find his ball in the long thick grass.
luggage*	the cases or bags you take on a journey
lump	a large piece; a swelling
lunch	a meal in the middle of the day **lunches**

luggage

machine

M m

machine*	a thing with moving parts built to do work, like a sewing-*machine* **machinery**
made	We *made* a cake. (past of *make*)
magazine*	a kind of newspaper with pictures and stories that comes out weekly or monthly
magic	making wonderful things appear or happen **magician**
magpie	a black and white bird with a long tail. (See picture on page 14.)
maid	a woman servant
main	most important

magazine

M m

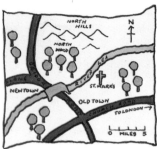

map

make	1. build; put together 2. cook 3. get somebody to do something **made, making**
man	A boy grows up to be a *man*. **men, fireman, postman**
manners	the way you behave
many	a lot. Tom has *many* toys.
map*	a drawing which shows where places are
marble	a little ball of glass you play with
March	the third month of the year
march	walk in step, like soldiers **marched, marches, marching**
margarine	a food that looks like butter
mark	1. the sign a teacher puts on your work to show how good it is 2. a spot or scratch
market*	a place with stalls where you can buy things
marmalade	jam made from oranges
marry	become a husband or wife **marriage, married, marries, marrying**
marvellous	wonderful
mass	1. a quantity; a heap 2. the amount of material in an object
mat	a small rug
match	1. You strike a *match* to get a flame. 2. a game played by two teams **matches**
material	what anything is made of
maths	learning about sums. *Maths* is short for **mathematics**.
mattress*	the soft part of a bed you lie on **mattresses**
May	the fifth month of the year

market

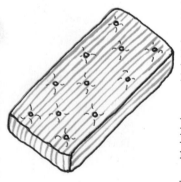

mattress

may	I *may* play if it stops raining.
mayor	the head person in a town **mayoress**
meal	the food you sit down to eat at a table. Lunch is a *meal*.
mean	1. selfish; unkind 2. Tom did not *mean* to break the plate, but it fell out of his hands. 3. The word 'mend' *means* 'repair'.
measles	an illness that gives you red spots
measure	find out how big or long. You *measure* some things with rulers or scales. **measured, measuring***
meat	the parts of animals that you eat
medicine*	You take *medicine* when you are ill, to make you better.
meet	1. see and talk to 2. join. The two roads *meet* here. **meeting, met**
melon	a large round fruit with green or yellow skin. (See picture on page 43.)
melt	heat a thing so that it goes soft **melted, melting**
men	more than one man
mend	put right; repair **mended, mending**
merry	happy; jolly
mess	when things are untidy; a muddle
message	the news you send to someone
met	I *met* Tom at school. (past of *meet*)
metal	a hard material like iron or steel
meter*	a machine which measures how much of something like electricity has been used
metre	100 centimetres make 1 *metre*. **metric**

measuring

medicine

meter

M m

mince pie

mirror

moat

mice	more than one *mouse*
midday	the middle of the day; twelve o'clock
middle	the centre; half-way
midnight	the middle of the night; twelve o'clock
might	I *might* go out if Tom would go too.
mile	a long way. 1,760 yards make 1 *mile*.
milk	a drink we get from cows **milkman**
mill	1. a factory where cloth is made 2. a place where flour is made
millimetre	1,000 *millimetres* make 1 metre.
million	the number 1,000,000
mince	chop into tiny pieces **minced, mincemeat, mince pie*, mincing**
mind	take care of. *Mind* the baby. **minded, minding**
mine	1. belonging to me. The toy is *mine*. 2. a deep hole were coal is dug
minus	take away. The sign for *minus* is −. 7 − 3 = 4.
minute	60 seconds make 1 *minute*. 60 *minutes* make 1 hour.
mirror*	a glass you look in to see yourself
miss	1. be sorry that someone is not here 2. not to catch something. You will *miss* the bus unless you run. 3. not to hit what you aim at 4. a woman who is not married **missed, misses, missing**
mistake	something wrong
mix	put different things together; stir **mixed, mixes, mixing, mixture**
moat*	a deep ditch round a castle
model	a small copy you make of something like an aeroplane or train

modern	new; happening now
mole	a small animal that digs long holes
Monday	the second day of the week
money	coins and notes. You use *money* to buy things.
monkey	an animal that lives in trees. (See picture on page 9.)
month	about 4 weeks. 12 *months* make 1 year.
moon	The *moon* shines in the sky at night.
moor	1. a large piece of rough land 2. tie up a boat to stop it moving
mop	a bundle of cloth at the end of a stick, used for cleaning
more	greater; a bigger number
morning	the early part of the day
most	biggest; largest
moth	an insect, like a butterfly. (See picture on page 53.)
mother	a woman who has children; mummy
motor	an engine that makes a car move **motor-car, motor-cycle*, motorist**
motorway*	a long wide road for cars and lorries to travel fast
mountain*	a very high hill
mouse	an animal like a small rat. (See picture on page 9.) **mice**
mouth	You put food in your *mouth* to eat. (See picture on page 17.)
move	1. take something from one place to another 2. not to stay still 3. go somewhere else to live **moved, moving**

motor-cycle

motorway

mountains

M m

mow	cut grass or corn **mowed, mowing**	
much	a lot. How *much* does the dress in the window cost?	
mud*	wet soil **muddy, mudguard**	
muddle	an untidy mess; when things are mixed up	
mug*	a kind of cup without a saucer	
mule	an animal something like a horse	
multiply	make something a number of times bigger **multiplication, multiplied, multiplying**	
mumble	not to speak clearly **mumbled, mumbling**	
mummy	a child's name for mother	
mumps	an illness that makes your face and neck swell	
murder	kill someone **murdered, murdering**	
muscle	I can feel the *muscle* in my arm helping me to lift a heavy load.	
museum	a place you visit to see interesting and unusual objects	
mushroom*	a plant you can eat. It is shaped like an umbrella and grows fast.	
music	sounds that you can sing or play. Play the piano so that we can dance to the *music*. **musical, musician**	
must	You *must* wash if you are dirty. **mustn't = must not**	
mustard	a yellow paste that tastes hot and is often eaten with meat	
mutton	meat from a sheep	
myself	I did the sum by *myself*.	

mud

mug

mushroom

nail	1. You hammer *nails* into wood. 2. the hard end of your finger or toe. (See picture on page 17.)
name	what anyone or anything is called
narrow	thin; not far from side to side
nasty	not pleasant; bad; horrid
nature	the world and the things in it, like animals and plants
naughty	bad; not behaving well
navy	a large number of ships and sailors
near	close; not far away
neat	tidy; clean
necessary	something that you need to do
neck	the narrow part of your body between your head and shoulders. (See picture on page 17.)
necklace*	a string of beads that girls sometimes wear round their necks
need	want badly; be without **needed, needing**
needle	a thin, pointed piece of metal used for sewing and knitting
neighbour	a person who lives near you
neither	not one or the other; not either
nest*	A bird makes a *nest* to lay eggs in.
net	You can catch butterflies with a *net*.
netball*	a game where you score by throwing a ball into a high net
never	not ever; at no time
new	not used before; fresh; not old
news	something which has just happened **newsagent, newspaper**
next	nearest; the one after

necklace

nest

netball

N n

north 1

notes 1

nurse

nib	the point of a pen
nice	pleasing; good; enjoyable
night	the time when it is dark
nine	the number 9 **ninth (9th), nineteen (19), ninety (90)**
nobody	no one; no person
nod	move your head up and down **nodded, nodding**
noise	a loud sound **noisy**
none	not one; not any
nonsense	something silly
north*	1. a point on the compass 2. Scotland is *north* of England.
nose	the part of your face you smell with. (See picture on page 17.)
note*	1. a musical sound 2. money made of paper 3. a very short letter **notebook**
nothing	not anything; none
notice	1. see or watch 2. a message put up on a wall to tell you something **noticed, noticing**
November	the eleventh month of the year
now	at present; at this time
nowhere	not anywhere; in no place
number	how many; a figure. 6 is a *number*.
nurse*	A *nurse* looks after people in hospital.
nursery	a school for very young children; a room where children play **nurseries**
nut	1. *Nuts* grow in shells on trees. 2. a piece of metal which you screw on a bolt

nylon	a material. Some stockings and tights and clothes are made of *nylon*.

O o

oak

oak*	a big tree on which acorns grow
oar	You use *oars* to row a boat.
obey	do as you are told **obedient, obeyed, obeying**
object	something you can see or touch
oblong	a shape like a book; a rectangle
ocean*	a large sea
o'clock	the time shown on a clock
October	the tenth month of the year
odd	1. 3, 5 and 7 are *odd* numbers. 2. different; not like others; strange
office*	a building where men and women work at desks
often	many times; again and again
oil	a liquid used for lighting and heating and to make machines and engines work
old	having lasted a long time; not new **older, oldest**
once	one time only; in the past
one	the number 1
onion	a vegetable with a bulb. (See picture on page 107.)
only	alone; no more than
open	not shut or locked **opened, opening**
opposite	1. very different. Hot is the *opposite* of cold. 2. on the other side

ocean

office

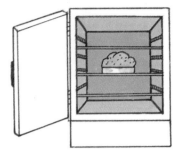

oven

overalls

packet

orange	1. a juicy fruit with pips. (See picture on page 43.) 2. a yellow and red colour like the fruit. (See picture on page 26.)
orchestra	a group of people playing music together
order	1. things in their right places 2. tell someone to do something **ordered, ordering**
ordinary	usual; not surprising
other	different; not this one
ought	You *ought* to clean your teeth.
ounce	a small weight or mass. 16 *ounces* make 1 pound.
ourselves	We make our beds *ourselves*.
out	not inside; not at home **outdoors, outside**
outing	a journey you enjoy
oven*	Food can be cooked or baked in an *oven*.
over	1. above; across; more than 2. ended. The holiday is *over*. **overalls*, overcoat**
owl	a large night bird with big eyes. (See picture on page 14.)
own	belonging to. Tom has his *own* bicycle. **owned, owner, owning**
ox	a large strong animal like a cow. (See picture on page 8.) **oxen**

P p

pack	1. put things into a box or parcel 2. a group or bundle **package, packed, packing**
packet*	a small parcel

pad	sheets of paper fastened together
paddle	walk in water with bare feet **paddled, paddling**
page	This is *page* 71 of this book.
pail	a bucket
pain	an ache; what you feel when you are hurt **painful**
paint	put colour on; make a picture
pair	a set of 2 things, like shoes; a couple
palace	a fine large house where a king lives
pale	light; without much colour
pan*	a flat dish for cooking in **pancake**
panda	a large black and white animal which looks like a bear. (See picture on page 8.)
pansy	a flower like a large violet. (See picture on page 41.) **pansies**
pant	breathe quickly when you are out of breath **panted, panting**
pantomime	a kind of play acted at Christmas
pants	clothes you wear next to your skin on the lower part of your body
paper	a thin material used for writing or printing on
parcel*	things wrapped in paper and tied up
parent	your mother or father
park*	a large space, often with trees, where you can play **parked, parking, car-park**
parrot	a bird with bright feathers. (See picture on page 14.)
part	a piece of something

pan

parcel

park

P p

party

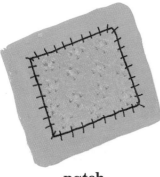

patch

pattern

party*	We all had a *party* on my birthday. **parties**	
pass	1. to hand to somebody 2. to go by 3. get through a test 4. a free ticket **passed, passes, passing, past**	
passage	a path; a corridor	
passenger	You are a *passenger* when you travel in a car or bus.	
past	before now; the time that has gone	
paste	1. a kind of glue used to stick things together 2. a soft food that you can spread	
pastry	the outside of a pie or tart, made with flour **pastries**	
pat	tap gently **patted, patting**	
patch*	a piece of material used to mend a hole **patches, patchwork**	
path	a place for walking **footpath**	
patient	A doctor helps a *patient* get better.	
pattern*	the way shapes are arranged in a drawing	
pavement	a path at the side of a road	
paw	an animal's foot	
pay	give money for something **paid, paying**	
pea	a small, round, green vegetable. (See picture on page 107.)	
peach	a juicy fruit with a stone. (See picture on page 43.) **peaches**	
pear	a juicy fruit with a core and pips. (See picture on page 43.)	
peck	A bird *pecks* food with its beak.	

pedal*	You press the *pedals* with your feet to make a bicycle go.
peel	take the skin off a fruit or vegetable **peeled, peeling**
peep	take a quick look at something when you think no one is looking **peeped, peeping**
peg	You hang clothes on a *peg*.
pen	You use a *pen* to write with ink.
pencil	You can write with a *pencil*. **pencil-case**
penguin	a sea bird that can swim but not fly. (See picture on page 14.)
penknife*	a small knife that folds up **penknives**
penny	1p. 100 *pence* make £1.00. **pence, pennies**
people	men, women and children
pepper	a powder with a hot taste
perhaps	possibly; it may be
person	a man, woman or child
pet	an animal that is kept at home
petal	the coloured part of a flower. (See picture on page 41.)
petrol	the liquid that makes the engine of a car work
photograph	a picture of people or places you want to remember. You take *photographs* with a camera. **photo, photographer**
piano*	a musical instrument which you play with your hands
pick	1. choose 2. gather things like fruit or flowers **picked, picking**

pedal

penknife

piano

P p

picnic*	a meal which you take to eat out of doors
picture	a drawing or photograph
pie	fruit or meat cooked in pastry
piece	a part of something; a bit
pig	a farm animal that grunts. (See picture on page 9.) **pig-sty**
pigeon	a grey bird often seen in towns. (See picture on page 14.)
pile	a heap; many things on top of each other
pill	medicine in a small ball which you swallow
pillow	a cushion. You rest your head on a *pillow* in bed.
pilot	A *pilot* flies an aeroplane.
pin	a sharp piece of wire to fasten things together
pinch	squeeze; grip with your fingers **pinched, pinches, pinching**
pine*	a tall tree with leaves which stay green all the year
pink	a pale red colour. (See picture on page 26.)
pint	a measure of liquids like milk equal to about half a litre. 8 *pints* = 1 gallon.
pip	a seed inside some fruits like apples and oranges
pipe	a kind of rod with a hole through the middle
pirate	A *pirate* robs ships at sea.
pistol	a small gun
pit	a deep hole in the ground
place	any spot; a town or village
plaice*	a flat fish

picnic

pine

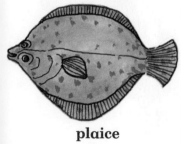

plaice

plain	1. clear; easy to see 2. land that is flat and has no hills
plait*	long hair twisted together
plane	a short word for aeroplane
planet	a large object in space like the earth that moves round the sun
plant	something that grows out of the ground
plastic	a strong light material that can be made into objects of any shape
Plasticine	a kind of clay for making models
plate	a flat dish to put food on
platform	1. stage; the high part in a hall 2. the part of a station where you get on the train
play	1. have a game 2. a story which is acted 3. make music on an instrument **played, player, playground, playing, playtime**
please	1. a word you use when you ask politely for something 2. make somebody happy **pleasant, pleased, pleasing, pleasure**
plenty	a lot; more than enough
plimsolls*	soft shoes you wear for running and playing games
plough	a machine used on a farm to dig the soil
plug	1. A *plug* keeps the water in a bath. 2. A *plug* fits into a special place in a wall where electricity can go into it.
plum	a fruit with a stone. (See picture on page 43.)
plus	Added to. The sign for *plus* is +. 6 + 2 = 8.
pocket*	a place in your clothes for carrying things

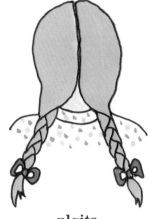

plaits

plimsolls

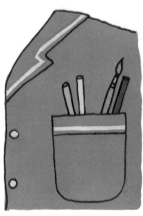

pocket

P p

pointing

pole

post office

poem	lines of words that often rhyme **poet, poetry**
point	1. a sharp end 2. show something with your finger **pointed, pointing***
poke	push the end of one thing into something else **poked, poker, poking**
pole*	a long thick stick
police	The job of the *police* is to stop people doing wrong and to catch those who have done wrong. **police-station, policeman, policewoman**
polish	make things shine **polished, polishes, polishing**
polite	behaving nicely; having good manners
pond	a small lake
pony	a small horse. (See picture on page 8.) **ponies**
pool	a puddle; a pond. A swimming *pool* has clean water in which you can swim.
poor	1. not having much money; not rich 2. badly done; not good
poppy	a bright red flower. (See picture on page 41.) **poppies**
pork	meat from a pig
porridge	a cooked food which some people eat for breakfast
port	a town that has docks
possible	might happen **possibly**
post	1. send off letters 2. a strong pole in the ground **posted, posting, postage, postcard, postman, post office*, post-box**

Pp

poster*	a large notice for people to see
pot	a bowl to hold liquid or to cook in
potato	a vegetable that grows under the ground. (See picture on page 107.) **potatoes**
pound	1. a sum of money. 100 pence make 1 *pound* (£1.00). 2. a weight or mass. 16 ounces make 1 *pound* (1 lb).
pour	1. rain heavily 2. You *pour* tea into a cup. **poured, pouring**
powder	dust; something broken into very tiny pieces
power	strength **powerful**
pram*	We take our baby out in a *pram*.
prayer	a message to God **pray, prayed, praying**
present*	1. here; not absent 2. something you give 3. now
press	push hard **pressed, presses, pressing**
pretend	play at being somebody else. Tom *pretends* he is a cowboy. **pretended, pretending**
pretty	nice to look at; pleasing **prettier, prettiest**
price	how much something costs
prickle	a thorn; a sharp point on a plant **prickly**
primary	first. Tom goes to a *primary* school.
primrose	a small yellow flower. (See picture on page 41.)
prince	the son of a king or queen

poster

pram

present 2

P p

prisoner

pudding

puppet

princess	the daughter of a king or queen **princesses**
printing	1. writing with big letters 2. making a book or newspaper with a machine
prison	a place where people who have done wrong are locked up **prisoner***
prize	something you get for winning or for doing good work
probable	likely to happen **probably**
programme	1. a list telling you what is going to happen in a concert or play 2. something you listen to on the radio or watch on television
promise	say you will do something and really mean it **promised, promising**
proper	right; correct
proud	very pleased with yourself
pudding*	a soft sweet food
puddle	a small pool of water
puff	blow out air or smoke **puffed, puffing**
pull	drag; tug something towards you **pulled, pulling**
pullover	a kind of sweater often with no sleeves
pump	a machine which pushes water or air into something **pumped, pumping**
punch	hit someone with your fist **punched, punches, punching**
puppet*	a doll you move with strings or your fingers
puppy	a young dog **puppies**

purple	a dark colour which you get by mixing red and blue. (See picture on page 26.)
purse*	a small bag for carrying money
push	press against; move something away from you **pushed, pushes, pushing**
puss	a cat
put	I *put* a coat on when it is cold. **putting**
puzzle	something which is hard to work out, like a jigsaw-*puzzle*
pyjamas*	a kind of suit you sleep in

purse

pyjamas

Q q

quack	the noise made by a duck
quantity	how many or how much of something
quarrel	an angry way of talking to someone when you do not agree **quarrelled, quarrelling**
quarter	$\frac{1}{4}$; what you get when you divide something into 4 equal parts
queen	a woman who is head of a country; the wife of a king
question	You ask a *question* when you want to know something.
queue*	people waiting in a line
quick	fast; going at great speed **quicker, quickest, quickly**
quiet	not making much sound; not noisy **quieter, quietest, quietly**
quite	mostly. I have *quite* a few toys.

queue

R r

rainbow

rabbit	a small furry animal with long ears. (See picture on page 9.)
race	run; try to go faster than others **raced, racing**
radio	a machine for listening to sounds. (See picture on page 51.)
rag	a piece of old cloth
rail	a bar made of wood or metal **railing**
railway	the track which trains run on
rain	drops of water that fall from the clouds **rained, raining**
rainbow*	the bright colours in the sky when the sun shines after rain
raincoat*	a coat that keeps you dry if it rains
rake*	a garden tool
ran	I *ran* to catch a bus. (past of *run*)
rang	Tom *rang* the bell. (past of *ring*)
raspberry	a small red fruit. (See picture on page 43.) **raspberries**
rat	an animal like a large mouse. (See picture on page 9.)
rattle	1. a baby's toy 2. the noise of things banging against each other **rattled, rattling**
raw	not cooked
razor	A man shaves hair off his face with a *razor*.
reach	arrive; come to a place **reached, reaches, reaching**
read	Ann likes to *read* a book in bed. **reading**
ready	waiting to start; waiting to be used

raincoat

rake

real	true; not made up **really**
reason	why you do something
record	You can hear music by playing *records* on a *record* player. **record player**
recorder*	a musical instrument you blow
recording	sounds, like music, taken down on a tape or disc
rectangle*	an oblong; a shape with corners like a square and 4 straight sides: two sides are longer than the other two
red	a colour like blood. (See picture on page 26.)
reel	Cotton is wound on a *reel*.
referee	a person who makes sure you keep to the rules in a game
refrigerator*	You keep food cool and fresh in a *refrigerator*.
refuse	to say no when you are asked to do something **refused, refusing**
reindeer	a kind of deer which lives in cold countries. (See picture on page 8.)
reins	leather straps used to guide a horse
remember	not to forget; keep a thing in your mind **remembered, remembering**
repair	mend. Ann used glue to *repair* the broken plate. **repaired, repairing**
repeat	do or say something again **repeated, repeating**
reply	answer a question **replied, replies, replying**
rescue	save someone from danger **rescued, rescuing**

recorder

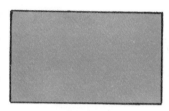

rectangle

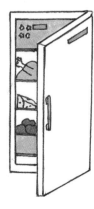

refrigerator

R r

rhubarb

ribbon

rifle

rest	1. the others 2. to be quiet; to lie down **rested, resting**
restaurant	a place where you can buy a meal; a café
return	1. come back; go back 2. give back what you have borrowed **returned, returning**
rhinoceros	a very big animal with a horn. *Rhino* is short for *rhinoceros*. (See picture on page 8.)
rhubarb*	a plant with thick red stalks
rhyme	'Tin' rhymes with 'bin'.
ribbon*	Ann ties her hair with a *ribbon*.
rice	white or brown seeds that are cooked to eat
rich	having a lot of money
riddle	a puzzle in words
ride	sit on a thing and be carried along **ridden, riding, rode**
rifle*	a long gun
right	1. good; true; not wrong 2. opposite of left
ring	1. the sound made by a bell 2. a circle. You can wear a *ring* on your finger. **rang, ringing, rung**
rip	tear something **ripped, ripping**
ripe	Fruit is *ripe* when it is ready to eat.
rise	get up; go higher **risen, rising, rose**
river	water that runs into a sea or lake
road	a wide path used by cars and buses
roar	a loud cry or noise like a lion makes **roared, roaring**

roast	cook in an oven
rob	steal **robbed, robber, robbing**
robin	a small bird with a red front. (See picture on page 14.)
rock*	1. a large stone 2. move gently from side to side **rocked, rocking**

rocks 1

rocket*	1. a kind of firework 2. a machine that is shot up into space
rod	a long thin bar of wood or metal
rode	Ann *rode* her bicycle. (past of *ride)*
roll	1. wind something like a bandage round and round 2. turn over and over 3. a small loaf of bread **rolled, roller, rolling, rolling-pin**
roof	the cover on top of house
room	1. a part of a building, like a bed*room* 2. enough space to keep things in
root	the part of a plant under the ground
rope	strong thick string; cord

rocket 1

rose	1. a flower with many petals that grows on a small bush. (See picture on page 41.) 2. got up (past of *rise)*
rough	1. uneven; not smooth 2. stormy
round	shaped like a circle or ball **roundabout, rounders, rounded**
row	1. a noisy quarrel 2. a line of people or things 3. move a boat with oars **rowed, rowing***

rowing 3

royal	to do with a king or queen
rub	You *rub* your hands to warm them. **rubbed, rubbing**

rucksack

rubber	You use a *rubber* to clean off pencil marks. Tyres are made of *rubber*.
rubbish	1. waste; things which you throw away 2. nonsense
rucksack*	a bag you carry on your back
rude	not polite; having bad manners
rug	a small carpet; a mat
ruler	1. a strip or wood used to measure things and to draw lines 2. the head of a country
run	move quickly on your feet **ran, runner, running**
runway	a road on which aeroplanes land at an airport
rush	hurry; move quickly **rushed, rushes, rushing**
rust	You often find *rust* on metal when it has got wet. **rusty**

S s

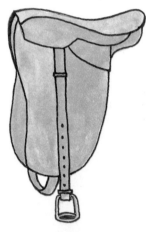

saddle

sack	a large strong bag
sad	unhappy
saddle*	a seat on a bicycle or horse
safe	not in danger; not likely to be hurt **safely, safety**
said	spoke (past of *say*)
sail	go on a journey by boat **sailed, sailing, sailor**
sale	a time or place for selling something
salmon*	a large pink fish
salt	a white powder sometimes used to make food more tasty

salmon

same	alike; not different
sand	light brown powder found on the beach
sandal	a shoe held on by straps
sandwich	two slices of bread with meat or some other food in the middle **sandwiches**
sang	We *sang* a carol. (past of *sing*)
sardine	a small fish. *Sardines* are sold in tins.
satchel*	a bag for carrying books to school
Saturday	the last day of the week
sauce	a thick liquid. You pour *sauce* over some food to make it more tasty.
saucepan	a dish with a long handle for cooking
saucer	a small dish to put a cup on
sausage	a food which has minced meat in it
save	1. get someone out of danger 2. keep things so that you can use them later. I *save* some of my pocket money every week. **saved, saving, savings**
saw	1. a tool used for cutting wood 2. I *saw* a crash yesterday. (past of *see*)
say	speak **said, saying**
scales	1. a weighing machine 2. sets of notes in music
scare	make someone afraid; frighten **scarecrow, scared, scaring**
scarf*	a piece of cloth you wear round your neck **scarves**
school	the building where you go to learn
science	finding out how things work and why things happen
scissors*	You use *scissors* for cutting.

satchel

scarf

scissors

S s

score	1. get a goal 2. the number of goals or runs on each side in a game
scout	Tom's big brother is a *Scout*.
scrape	clean something with a knife **scraped, scraping**
scratch	a small cut on your skin **scratched, scratches, scratching**
scream	give a loud cry when you are hurt or frightened **screamed, screaming**
screw*	a kind of nail
scribble	write quickly and carelessly **scribbled, scribbling**
scrub	rub something hard with a brush to clean it **scrubbed, scrubbing**
sea	the salt water round the land **seashore, seaside, seaweed**
search	look carefully for something **searched, searches, searching**
seat	A *seat* is made to sit on. **seat-belt***
second	1. 2nd; the one after the first 2. a very short time. 60 *seconds* make 1 minute. **secondary**
secret	something you know that you do not want others to know
see	You *see* things with your eyes. **saw, seeing, seen**
seed	Plants grow from *seeds*.
seek	look for; try to find
seem	appear to be; look as if
seesaw*	a toy that you ride up and down on

screw

seat-belt

seesaw

selfish	greedy; thinking too much about what you want for yourself
sell	get money for a thing. Butchers *sell* meat. **selling, sold**
send	I shall *send* Tom a birthday card. **sending, sent**
September	the ninth month of the year
serve	1. sell things in a shop 2. give out food **servant, served, service, serving**
set	1. put things in the right place 2. a group of things together **setting**
settee*	a long, soft seat
seven	the number 7 **seventh (7th), seventeen (17), seventy (70)**
sew	use a needle and cotton **sewed, sewing, sewing-machine, sewn**
shade	1. a cover over a light 2. a place which is not bright **shaded, shading, shadow*, shady**
shake	move a thing up and down or from side to side quickly **shaken, shaking, shook**
shall	We *shall* go home after school. **shan't = shall not**
shape	the picture you make if you draw a line round anything
share	divide; split something into parts and give them away **shared, sharing**
sharp	pointed; good to cut with; not blunt
shave	cut hair off the face with a razor **shaved, shaving**
shed*	a wooden hut

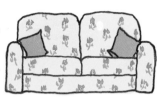

settee

shadow

shed

S s

	sheep	an animal covered with wool. (See picture on page 9.) **shepherd**
	sheet	1. a large piece of cloth on a bed 2. a piece of paper
	**shelf***	a flat board to keep things on **shelves, bookshelf**
	shell	a hard cover, like an egg*shell*
shelf	**shelter***	a place which keeps the rain off
	shine	be bright; give out light **shining, shiny, shone, sunshine**
	ship	a big boat
	shirt	Boys and men wear *shirts*.
	**shiver**	shake because you are cold or frightened **shivered, shivering**
	shock	a nasty surprise **shocking**
	shoe	You wear *shoes* on your feet.
shelter	**shone**	The sun *shone* all day yesterday. (past of *shine*)
	shook	I *shook* the bottle. (past of *shake*)
	shoot	fire a gun **shooting, shot**
	shop	a place where things are sold **shopkeeper, shopping**
	**shore**	land at the side of water; a beach
	short	not long or tall
	shorts*	short trousers
	should	I *should* like a new bicycle. **shouldn't = should not**
	shoulder	the joint between your arm and body. (See picture on page 17.)
shorts	**shout**	call out; speak loudly **shouted, shouting**

shovel*	a kind of small spade
show	let someone see something; explain **showed, showing, shown**
shower*	1. when it rains for a short time 2. a bath when you stand under water
shut	closed; not open
sick	not feeling well; ill **sickness**
side	1. the part not at the top or bottom; the edge 2. a team in a game **sideways, seaside, sideboard.**
sign	1. a notice that tells you something 2. write your name **signal, signed, signing, signpost**
silk	soft, shiny cloth
sill	the shelf at the bottom of a window
silly	stupid; not clever **sillier, silliest**
silver	a shiny metal that costs a lot
simple	easy; not hard to do
since	I have been ill *since* Monday.
sing	make music with your voice **sang, singer, singing, sung**
sink*	1. a place in the kitchen for washing up 2. go down under water **sank, sinking, sunk**
sister	a girl who has the same mother and father as you
sit	You *sit* on a chair. **sat, sitting**
six	the number 6 **sixth (6th), sixteen (16), sixty (60)**
size	how big a thing is

shovel

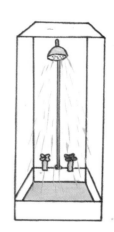

shower 2

sink 1

S s

skating

skipping

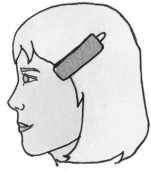

slide 1

skate	move along on ice; slide **skated, skating***
skeleton	the bony part of your body
skin	Your body is covered with *skin*.
skip	jump over a rope which is turning **skipped, skipping***
skirt	Girls and women wear *skirts*.
sky	the space above the earth. The sunset turned the *sky* red and gold. **skies**
slap	hit someone with your hand; smack **slapped, slapping**
sleep	rest in bed, with your eyes closed **sleeping, sleepy, slept**
sleeve	the part of your clothes which covers your arm
slice	a thin, flat piece cut off something
slide*	1. a small comb that keeps the hair tidy 2. move easily over smooth ground **slid, sliding**
slip	nearly fall over **slipped, slippery, slipping**
slipper	a soft shoe you wear in the house
slow	taking a long time; not quick
smack	hit someone with your hand; slap **smacked, smacking**
small	little; not big **smaller, smallest**
smart	well-dressed; tidy
smash	break a thing into bits; crash **smashed, smashes, smashing**
smell	You use your nose to *smell* with. **smelling, smelt**
smile	look happy and pleased **smiled, smiling**

smoke	*Smoke* rises from a burning fire. **smoked, smoking, smoky**
smooth	flat and polished; not rough
snail	a small animal with a shell. (See picture on page 9.)
snake	a long thin animal that slides along the ground and can be dangerous. (See picture on page 9.)
snatch	grab; take something quickly **snatched, snatches, snatching**
sneeze	make a sudden loud noise with your nose **sneezed, sneezing**
snore	breathe noisily while you are asleep **snored, snoring**
snow	soft white flakes that fall in winter **snowball, snowed, snowing, snowflake, snowman***
snowdrop	a small, white flower. (See picture on page 41.)
soap	You wash with *soap* and water.
sock*	You wear *socks* on your feet.
soft	1. not hard. Wool is *soft* to touch. 2. quiet; not loud **softer, softest, softly**
soil	the ground or earth
sold	Dad *sold* his car. (past of *sell*)
soldier*	a man or woman in an army
some	a few; a number; not all **somebody, somehow, someone, something, sometimes, somewhere**
son	a boy child
song	a piece of music with words
soon	in a short time; quickly
sore	painful; hurting
sorry	I am *sorry* I broke a cup.

snowman

socks

soldier

S s

sort	a kind; a set of things that are alike
sound	a noise; something that you can hear
soup	a hot liquid food made from meat or vegetables
sour	not sweet; with a bitter taste. A lemon tastes *sour*.
south*	1. a point on the compass 2. London is in the *south* of England.
sow	1. a kind of pig 2. put seeds in the ground **sowed, sowing, sown**

south 1

space	1. an empty place; room for things 2. far above the earth. The rocket was sent into *space* to find a new planet. **spacecraft*, spaceship**
spade	a tool used for digging. The gardener dug the ground with a *spade*.
spare	left over; not needed; extra
spark	a burning bit of the fire that flies out
sparrow	a small bird that lives near houses. (See picture on page 14.)
speak	talk; use your voice **speaker, speaking, spoke, spoken**

spacecraft

spear	a pointed stick used long ago for fighting
special	unusual; not ordinary
speed	how fast something goes
spell	give the letters of a word in order **spelling, spelt**
spend	pay out money. Ann *spent* her pocket money buying Christmas presents. **spending, spent**
spider*	a tiny animal with 8 legs. A *spider* spins a web.
spill	upset a liquid or food; tip over **spilled, spilling, spilt**

spider

spin	1. turn something round quickly, like a top; twist 2. make threads **spinning, spun**
splash	throw water about **splashed, splashes, splashing**
split	break something from end to end **splitting**
spoil	make something go bad **spoiled, spoiling, spoilt**
spoke	talked (past of *speak*)
sponge*	a soft thing that holds water. You use a *sponge* for washing.
spoon	You sometimes eat with a *spoon*. You stir things with a *spoon*.
sport	fun; a game you play, like football
spot	a small mark **spotted**
spout*	the part of a teapot or kettle for pouring out
spread	press something out flat, like butter on bread; cover
spring	1. the time of year between winter and summer 2. jump 3. a small stream of water 4. a piece of metal that goes back into place after you have pressed it **sprang, springing, springy, sprung**
spy	A *spy* tries to find out secrets. **spies**
square*	a shape with 4 equal sides
squash	1. press flat; squeeze 2. a drink made with fruit **squashed, squashes, squashing**
squeak	make a tiny sound like a mouse **squeaked, squeaking**

sponge

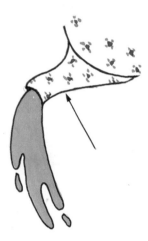

spout

square

stable

stamps

stars 1

squeal	make a long, high noise when you are frightened **squealed, squealing**
squeeze	press hard; squash **squeezed, squeezing**
squirrel	an animal with a bushy tail. (See picture on page 9.)
stable*	A horse is kept in a *stable*.
stage	the high part of a hall floor where plays are acted; a platform
stairs	the steps inside a building. (See picture on page 51.) **staircase, downstairs, upstairs**
stalk	the thin stem of a plant. (See picture on page 41.)
stall	a kind of shop in a market
stamp*	You stick a *stamp* on a letter to pay for sending it by post. **stamp-album**
stand	to be on your feet; not to sit **standing, stood**
star*	1. a tiny light shining in the sky at night 2. a well-known singer or actor
stare	look very hard at something, with your eyes wide open **stared, staring**
start	begin; set out **started, starting**
station	1. the place where a train stops 2. a building where some people work, like a police-*station* or fire-*station*
stay	stop in one place; not to go away **stayed, staying**
steal	take a thing which is not yours; rob **stealing, stole, stolen**
steam	*Steam* rises from boiling water. **steamed, steamer, steaming**

steel	a very strong metal, made from iron
steep	hard to climb; rising sharply
steeple*	the pointed top of a church
stem	a thick stalk; the main part of a plant above the ground
step	1. put one foot in front of the other when walking 2. a part of a staircase; one stair **stepped, stepping, footstep**
stereo*	sound coming from two different places at the same time
stick	1. a long piece of wood; a rod 2. fasten with glue **sticking, sticky, stuck**
still	1. not moving; keeping quiet 2. Tom ate a lot but was *still* hungry.
sting	a sharp point stuck into you by an insect or a plant **stinging, stung**
stir	move something round and round. Daddy *stirs* his tea with a spoon. **stirred, stirring**
stitch	sew with a needle **stitched, stitches, stitching**
stocking	People wear *stockings* to cover their legs and feet.
stole	robbed (past of *steal*)
stomach	a part inside your body. The food you eat goes into your *stomach*.
stone	1. a small piece of rock 2. the hard part inside some fruits **stony**
stool*	a seat without a back
stop	end what you are doing; not to go on **stopped, stopper, stopping**

steeple

stereo

stool

S s

store	1. a large shop that sells many things 2. keep; save up	
storm	bad weather, with wind and rain	
story	a tale. I read a *story* in the book. **stories**	
straight	1. not bent or crooked 2. neat and tidy	
strange	odd; surprising	
stranger	someone you have not seen before	
strap*	a long, thin piece of leather	
straw*	1. dried stalks of corn 2. a thin kind of pipe you use for drinking	
strawberry	a small red fruit. (See picture on page 43.) **strawberries**	
stream	a small river; a large brook	
street	a road in a town	
stretch	make something longer or wider by pulling it **stretched, stretching**	
strike	1. hit; give a blow 2. refuse to work **striking, struck**	
string	You use *string* for tying up parcels.	
strip	1. a long, thin piece 2. take off your clothes **stripped, stripping**	
stripe*	a thin band of colour	
stroke	rub a thing gently with your hand **stroked, stroking**	
strong	fit and well; not weak **strength, stronger, strongest**	
stuck	fastened (past of *stick*)	
stuff	cloth; what anything is made of	
stupid	silly; not clever	

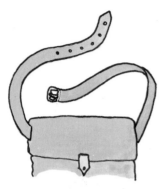

strap

straw 2

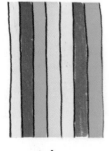

stripes

sty*	A pig lives in a *sty*. **sties, pig-sty**
subtract	take away from **subtracted, subtracting, subtraction**
such	so much. It was *such* a wet day that we had to stay in the house.
suck	You can *suck* milk through a straw. **sucked, sucking**
suddenly	all at once; quickly
sugar	a white powder used to make food or drink sweet
suit	a set of clothes
sum*	1. You work out *sums* in arithmetic. 2. the answer you get when you add figures together
summer	the time of year between spring and autumn
sun	The *sun* shines in the sky and gives us light and heat. **sunbathe, sunny, sunrise, sunset, sunshine**
Sunday	the first day of the week
supermarket	a large shop where many things are sold
supper	the last meal of the day
suppose	believe; think that something is true **supposed, supposing**
sure	knowing you are right; certain
surprise	something which happens that you did not expect **surprised, surprising**
swallow	1. a bird that catches insects as it flies. (See picture on page 14.) 2. let food or drink go down your throat **swallowed, swallowing**
swan*	a large white water bird
sweater	a knitted pullover with sleeves

sty

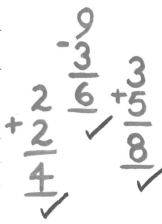

sums 1

swan

switch

tadpoles

tambourine

sweep	1. brush things up with a broom 2. a man who cleans chimneys **sweeping, swept**
sweet	with a sugary taste, like toffee
swell	grow bigger or fatter **swelled, swelling, swollen**
swim	move along in the water, using your arms and legs **swam, swimming, swum**
swing	1. We play on the *swings* in the park. 2. move from one side to the other **swinging, swung**
switch*	You press a *switch* to turn on an electric light. **switches**
sword	a long sharp knife for fighting
syrup	a sweet, sticky liquid, like treacle

T t

table	a piece of furniture with a flat top on legs. (See picture on page 51.) **tablecloth**
tadpole*	A *tadpole* turns into a frog.
tail	A dog wags its *tail*.
tailor	A *tailor* makes clothes.
take	hold; carry **taken, taking, took**
tale	a story you are told
talk	speak; say **talked, talking**
tall	high. Most trees grow *tall*.
tambourine*	a kind of small drum
tame	not fierce or wild; gentle

tank	a large holder for petrol or water
tap	1. You turn a *tap* on to get water. 2. hit gently **tapped, tapping**
tape	a special ribbon for taking down sound
tape-recorder*	a machine for recording sound and playing it back
tart	pastry, with jam or fruit on it
taste	You *taste* food with your tongue. **tasted, tasting, tasty**
taxi	a car you pay to ride in
tea	1. a hot drink 2. a meal in the afternoon **teapot, teaspoon, teatime**
teach	give lessons; explain something **taught, teacher, teaches, teaching**
team	a group of players; a side in a game
tear	1. When you cry, *tears* drop from your eyes. 2. pull to pieces; rip **tearing, tore, torn**
teeth	more than one tooth. (See picture on page 17.)
telephone*	You use a *telephone* to talk to someone a long way away.
television*	a machine that gives pictures and sounds. **TV** is short for *television*. (See picture on page 51.)
tell	say; give news to someone **telling, told**
temperature	the amount of heat
ten	the number 10 **tenth (10th)**
tennis	a game for 2 or 4 players with special bats and balls
tent	People go camping in *tents*.

tape-recorder

telephone

television

Tt

theatre

terrible	awful; very bad
test	Teacher gives us a *test* to find out what we know.
thank	You say '*Thank* you' to someone who has been nice to you.
that	I hope *that* you can come to tea.
theatre*	a building where plays are acted
their	belonging to them
them	I like books and often read *them*.
then	1. at that time 2. afterwards
there	in that place; not here
thermometer*	You use a *thermometer* to find out how hot or cold something or someone is.
these	the ones that are here
they	Tom and Ann said *they* would play.
thick	wide; not thin; crowded together
thief	someone who steals; a robber **thieves**
thimble*	You wear a *thimble* to cover your finger when you are sewing.
thin	narrow; not fat; not thick **thinner, thinnest**
thing	*Thing* is a name for whatever you can see or touch.
think	believe. I *think* books are useful. *Think* hard before you answer. **thinking, thought**
third	3rd; the one after the second
thirsty	wanting a drink
thirteen	the number 13
thirty	the number 30
this	*This* book is a dictionary.

thermometer

thimble

thistle*	a plant with prickles
thorn*	a sharp point on the stem of a plant. Roses have sharp *thorns* on their stems.
those	the ones that are there. I like *those* toys in the shop.
though	even if; although. Ann took her umbrella even *though* the sun was shining.
thought	believed (past of *think*)
thousand	the number 1,000
thread	strong cotton used for sewing. Sew on the buttons using *thread*.
three	the number 3
throat	the inside of the front part of your neck. You swallow food down your *throat*.
throne*	a special chair for a very important person like a king or queen
through	from one end to the other. Tom looked *through* the keyhole.
throw	send something through the air. We *throw* the ball to each other. **threw, throwing, thrown**
thrush	a spotted bird which sings sweetly. (See picture on page 14.) **thrushes**
thumb	the short, thick finger on your hand. (See picture on page 17.)
thunder	the loud noise in the sky in a storm. The flash of lightning is followed by the sound of *thunder*.
Thursday	the fifth day of the week
tick	1. the sound made by a watch or clock 2. a mark to show your work is right
ticket	a small card which shows that you have paid
tickle	touch someone lightly to make him laugh **tickled, tickling**
tidy	neat; in the right order

thistle

thorns

throne

T t

tie 2

tiles

tomato

tie*	1. fasten; make a knot 2. a strip of cloth worn with a collar **tied, ties, tying**
tiger	a fierce animal with stripes. (See picture on page 8.)
tights	long stockings which fit closely over the legs and the lower part of your body
tile*	a kind of thin, flat brick
time	the hours and minutes which the clock shows **daytime, night-time, playtime**
tin	a metal box or can; a shiny metal
tiny	very small
tip	1. a pointed end, like a finger-tip 2. turn over; pour out **tipped, tipping**
tired	sleepy; wanting to rest
tissue	thin, soft paper
toad	an animal like a frog. (See picture on page 9.)
toast	You make *toast* by heating slices of bread. **toaster**
today	this day
toe	You have 5 *toes* on your foot. (See picture on page 17.)
toffee	a sweet made of sugar and butter
together	with others. We all play *together*.
toilet	a lavatory; a W.C.
told	said (past of *tell*)
tomato*	a red fruit you eat as a vegetable **tomatoes**
tomorrow	the day after today
ton	a heavy weight or mass. 2,240 pounds make 1 *ton*.

tongue	the part in your mouth that moves
tonight	this night; the end of today
tonne	1,000 kilograms make 1 *tonne*.
took	carried (past of *take*)
tool	You use a *tool* to work with.
tooth	A *tooth* is used for biting. (See picture on page 17.) **teeth, toothache, toothbrush, toothpaste**
top	1. the highest part 2. a toy that you spin
torch*	an electric light you can carry about **torches**
torn	ripped (past or *tear*)
tortoise	a very slow animal with a shell. (See picture on page 9.)
touch	put your hand on; feel gently **touched, touches, touching**
towel	a cloth you dry with
tower*	a tall, narrow building
town	a place where many people live; a lot of houses and shops
toy	A *toy* is a thing a child plays with.
trace	copy a picture or map by drawing over it on thin paper **traced, tracing**
track	1. a rough, narrow patch 2. railway lines 3. a rounded path for racing
tractor*	a machine on a farm to pull loads
traffic	things travelling on the roads **traffic lights**
train	carriages pulled by an engine
trap	We caught a mouse in a *trap*.

torch

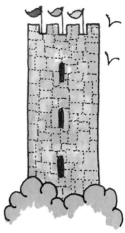

tower

tractor

T t

travel	make a journey; go from place to place **travelled, traveller, travelling**
tray	You carry things on a *tray*.
treacle	a dark, sweet, sticky liquid
treasure	a lot of jewels or gold
treat	a special outing or food that you enjoy
tree	a large plant with a trunk and branches
triangle	1. a shape with 3 sides 2. a musical instrument which you tap
trick	something clever done to amuse you
trip	1. a short journey; an outing 2. almost fall over **tripped, tripping**
trot	run slowly **trotted, trotting**
trousers*	People wear *trousers* to cover their legs.
truck	a lorry
true	right; correct; real
trumpet*	a musical instrument which you blow
trunk*	1. a large box or case 2. the thick part of a tree 3. the long nose of an elephant
try	I *try* to get my sums right. **tried, tries, trying**
tub	a deep wooden or plastic bowl
Tuesday	the third day of the week
tug	1. give a sudden pull 2. a boat that pulls other boats along **tugboat, tugged, tugging**
tulip	a flower with a long stem. (See picture on page 41.)
tumble	fall over **tumbled, tumbling**
tummy	a child's word for stomach

trousers

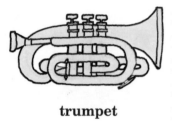

trumpet

trunk 3

Tt/Uu

tune	a piece of music
tunnel*	a passage dug through the ground
turkey*	a large farm bird. Some people eat *turkey* at Christmas.
turn	1. move. I *turn* the pages of my book. 2. go a different way. I *turn* the corner. 3. change. Tadpoles *turn* into frogs. **turned, turning**
twelve	the number 12
twenty	the number 20
twice	2 times
twig	a small branch of a tree
twin	one of 2 babies born together
twist	turn round and round; spin; wind **twisted, twisting**
two	the number 2
type	print letters and figures with a machine **typed, typing, typist, typewriter**
tyre	the rubber part round a wheel

tunnel

turkey

U u

ugly	not nice to look at **uglier, ugliest**
umbrella*	An *umbrella* keeps the rain off.
uncle	your mother's or father's brother; your aunt's husband
under	below; less than **underneath**
understanding	know what something means **understanding, understood**
undo	untie; open **undid, undoes, undoing, undone**

umbrella

U u / V v

uniform

van

vase

undress	take your clothes off **undressed, undressess, undressing**	
unhappy	sad; not happy	
uniform*	the clothes worn by people like nurses and soldiers	
universe	everything that is on the Earth and in space **universal**	
unless	if not. I shall be late *unless* I hurry.	
unlucky	when things do not go right for you; not lucky	
untidy	not neat; not tidy	
until	We play outside *until* it is dark.	
unusual	something you do not expect to happen or to see; not usual	
upside-down	the wrong way up	
upstairs	the rooms above in a building. (See picture on page 51.)	
use	I *use* a pencil to write with. **used, useful, useless, user, using**	
usual	often done **usually**	

V v

valley	low land between hills or mountains
van*	a car for carrying things
vanish	disappear suddenly; become invisible
vase*	a jar to hold flowers
vegetable	a plant that you eat. (See picture on page 107.)
vehicle	a thing that moves along on wheels
verse	a part of a poem

Vegetables

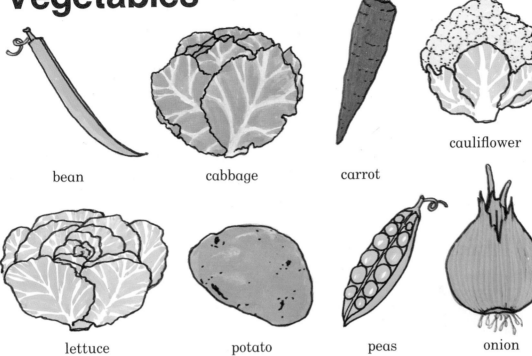

bean   cabbage   carrot   cauliflower

lettuce   potato   peas   onion

very	much; greatly. I am *very* happy.
vest	clothes you wear next to your skin on the top part of your body
video	You use a *video* tape to record anything you want to see later on your television set.
village	a group of houses in the country
violet	a small, purple wild flower
violin*	a musical instrument played with a bow
visit	go to see someone; go somewhere **visited, visiting, visitor**
voice	the sound you make when you speak or sing
volume	1. an amount of space or sound 2. a book

violin

107

W w

wag	shake. A dog *wags* its tail. **wagged, wagging**	
wagon*	1. a cart with 4 wheels 2. a railway truck	
waist	the narrow middle part of your body. (See picture on page 17.)	
wait	stay until something happens **waited, waiting**	
waiter*	A *waiter* brings your food in a café or restaurant. **waitress, waitresses**	
wake	stop sleeping. I *wake* up early. **waken, waking, woke**	
walk	go on foot **walked, walking**	
wall	the side of a room or building. (See picture on page 51.)	
want	wish to have. I *want* a book to read. **wanted, wanting**	
war	a fight between countries	
wardrobe*	a cupboard to keep your clothes in	
warm	fairly hot. It is *warm* by the fire.	
warn	tell you about the danger if you do something **warned, warning**	
was	Ann *was* ill, but she is better now. (past of *is*) **wasn't**	
wash	clean with water. I always *wash* before I eat. **washed, washes, washing**	
wasp	an insect like a bee which stings. (See picture on page 53.)	
waste	use without care; spoil; throw away **wasted, wasting**	

wagon 1

waiter

wardrobe

W w

watch*	1. a small clock worn on the wrist 2. look at something carefully 3. look after something; guard **watched, watches, watching**
water	You can get *water* from the tap. Rain is made of *water*.
wave	1. the high, moving part of the water in the sea 2. move something up and down. You *wave* your hand. **waved, waving**
wavy	curly. Ann has *wavy* hair.
way	1. a road or path 2. how to do something
weak	not strong; not fit **weaker, weakest, weakness**
wear	have clothes on; be dressed in **wearing, wore, worn**
weather	Tom and Ann like sunny *weather*, so that they can play in the park.
web	a net made by a spider
wedding*	a man and woman getting married
Wednesday	the fourth day of the week
weed	a wild plant that grows anywhere
week	7 days make 1 *week*. 52 *weeks* make 1 year.
weekend	Saturday and Sunday
weep	cry **weeping, wept**
weigh	find out how heavy a thing is or how much mass it has **weighed, weighing, weight**
well*	1. feeling fine; healthy; not ill 2. a deep hole with water or oil in it
went	moved; left (past of *go*). Ann *went* home after the party.

watch 1

wedding

well 2

W w

west 1

wheat

wheelbarrow

were	Tom and Ann *were* at my party. (past of *is*) **weren't**
west*	1. a point on the compass 2. The sun goes down in the *west*.
wet	damp; not dry; covered with water **wetter, wettest**
whale	a very large sea animal that looks like a fish. (See picture on page 8.)
what	*What* time is it? I saw *what* he did.
wheat*	a kind of corn used to make flour
wheel	a ring. Cars move on *wheels*. **wheelbarrow***
where	in what place. *Where* is he going?
which	*Which* toy do you like best? I like the toy *which* you gave me.
while	I sing *while* I wash.
whisper	speak very quietly; say softly **whispered, whispering**
whistle	1. make a sharp noise by blowing through your lips 2. The referee blows a *whistle* in a football game. **whistled, whistling**
white	a colour like milk. (See picture on page 26.)
who	*Who* is at the door? It was Tom *who* broke the plate. **whom, whose**
whole	all; not in parts
why	*Why* were you late?
wicked	bad; doing wrong
wide	a long way from one side to the other; not narrow **wider, widest**
width	how wide something is

wife	a woman who is married **wives**
wild	1. not tame. A lion is a *wild* animal. 2. not looked after. *Wild* plants grow in the woods.
will	*Will* you walk to school with me? Yes, I *will*. **won't = will not**
win	be first in a race **winner, winning, won**
wind	1. twist and turn. You *wind* a clock. **winding, wound** 2. air blowing about. The *wind* blew the leaves off the tree. **windmill*, windy**
window	A *window* is made out of glass and is put into the wall of a building. (See picture on page 51.) **window-sill**
wine	a drink made from the juice of grapes
wing	A bird uses its *wings* to fly.
winter*	the time of year between autumn and spring **wintry**
wipe	dry or clean a thing; rub the dirt off **wiped, wiping**
wire	a thread made of metal
wise	clever; knowing a lot
wish	hope very much for a thing; want **wished, wishes, wishing**
witch*	a woman in stories who does wicked things by magic **witches**
with	I go to school *with* Ann and John. **without**
wizard	a man in a fairy story who does magic
woke	Tom *woke* up early. (past of *wake*)

windmill 2

winter

witch

W w

wolf	a fierce wild animal that looks like a very big dog. (See picture on page 9.) **wolves**
woman	A girl grows up to be a *woman*. **women**
wonderful	marvellous; very good
wood*	1. the trunks and branches of trees 2. a small forest **wooden, woodwork**
wool*	the soft fur of a sheep. Some clothes are made of *wool*. **woollen, woolly**
word	a group of letters. 'Book' is a *word*.
wore	Ann *wore* a new hat. (past of *wear*)
work	a job you have to do **worked, working**
world	the earth. There are many countries in the *world*.
worm*	a small animal with no legs
would	Ann *would* come to tea if you invited her. **wouldn't = would not**
wound	1. hurt 2. twisted round (past of *wind*)
wrap	cover with paper; make a parcel **wrapped, wrapping**
wrist	the joint between your hand and arm. (See picture on page 17.)
write	put words on paper **writing, written, wrote**
wrong	not right; with mistakes

wood

wool

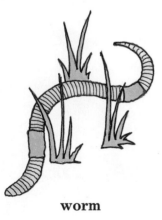

worm

yacht*	a small sailing boat
yard	1. a piece of ground with walls around it 2. an old measure. 1 *yard* is equal to a little less than 1 metre.
yawn	open your mouth wide when you are sleepy **yawned, yawning***
year	12 months; 52 weeks; 365 days
yellow	a colour like a ripe banana. (See picture on page 26.)
yesterday	the day before today
yet	till now. It is not *yet* dark, and I can still see to read.
yolk	the yellow part of an egg
you	How old are *you*?
young	not old; not grown up
your	What is *your* name? **yours, yourself, yourselves**

yacht

Z z

zebra	an animal with black and white stripes that looks like a horse. (See picture on page 8.)
zero	the number 0; nothing
zip	You slide a *zip* to do up your clothes. **zip-fastener**
zoo*	a park where wild animals are kept

yawning

zoo

Numbers

1	one	first
2	two	second
3	three	third
4	four	fourth
5	five	fifth
6	six	sixth
7	seven	seventh
8	eight	eighth
9	nine	ninth
10	ten	tenth
11	eleven	eleventh
12	twelve	twelfth
13	thirteen	thirteenth
14	fourteen	fourteenth
15	fifteen	fifteenth
16	sixteen	sixteenth
17	seventeen	seventeenth
18	eighteen	eighteenth
19	nineteen	nineteenth
20	twenty	twentieth
30	thirty	thirtieth
40	forty	fortieth
50	fifty	fiftieth
60	sixty	sixtieth
70	seventy	seventieth
80	eighty	eightieth
90	ninety	ninetieth
100	hundred	hundredth
1,000	thousand	thousandth
1,000,000	million	millionth

Girls' names

Alice	Helen	Marion
Alison	Irene	Marjorie
Angela	Jacqueline	Mary
Ann	Jane	Maureen
Anna	Janet	Mollie
Anne	Jean	Pamela
Barbara	Jennifer	Patricia
Betty	Jill	Pauline
Carol	Joan	Rachel
Caroline	Joy	Rosemary
Catherine	Joyce	Ruth
Daisy	Judith	Sally
Diana	Judy	Sandra
Diane	Julia	Sarah
Dora	June	Sheila
Eileen	Karen	Shirley
Elizabeth	Kate	Stella
Emma	Laura	Susan
Eva	Lilian	Sylvia
Frances	Linda	Tracy
Gillian	Louise	Valerie
Grace	Lucy	Wendy
Hazel	Margaret	Yvonne

Boys' names

Adam	Gordon	Norman
Alan	Graham	Oliver
Alec	Harold	Patrick
Andrew	Harry	Paul
Anthony	Henry	Peter
Barry	Hugh	Philip
Ben	Ian	Ralph
Benjamin	Jack	Raymond
Bill	James	Richard
Bob	Joe	Robert
Brian	John	Robin
Charles	Jonathan	Roger
Clive	Joseph	Ronald
Colin	Julian	Roy
Daniel	Keith	Sidney
David	Kenneth	Simon
Denis	Leonard	Stanley
Derek	Leslie	Stephen
Douglas	Lionel	Steven
Edgar	Mark	Thomas
Edward	Martin	Tom
Eric	Matthew	Trevor
Frank	Maurice	Victor
Fred	Michael	Walter
Gary	Neil	William
Geoffrey	Noel	Winston
George		
Gerald		

Places and peoples

Afghanistan	Afghans
Africa	Africans
Algeria	Algerians
America	Americans
Argentina	Argentinians
Asia	Asians
Australia	Australians
Austria	Austrians
Bangladesh	Bangladeshis
Belgium	Belgians
Bolivia	Bolivians
Brazil	Brazilians
Britain	British
Bulgaria	Bulgarians
Burma	Burmese
Canada	Canadians
Chile	Chileans
China	Chinese
Colombia	Colombians
Cuba	Cubans
Cyprus	Cypriots
Czechoslovakia	Czechoslovaks
Denmark	Danes
Egypt	Egyptians
England	English
Ethiopia	Ethiopians
Europe	Europeans
Finland	Finns
France	French
Germany	Germans
Ghana	Ghanaians
Greece	Greeks
Holland	Dutch
Hungary	Hungarians
Iceland	Icelanders
India	Indians
Indonesia	Indonesians
Iran	Iranians
Iraq	Iraqis
Ireland	Irish
Israel	Israelis
Italy	Italians

Places and peoples

Jamaica	Jamaicans
Japan	Japanese
Jordan	Jordanians
Kenya	Kenyans
Korea	Koreans
Lebanon	Lebanese
Libya	Libyans
Malaysia	Malaysians
Malta	Maltese
Mexico	Mexicans
Morocco	Moroccans
Netherlands	Dutch
New Zealand	New Zealanders
Nigeria	Nigerians
Norway	Norwegians
Pakistan	Pakistanis
Peru	Peruvians
Poland	Poles
Portugal	Portuguese
Romania	Romanians
Russia	Russians
Scotland	Scots
South Africa	South Africans
Spain	Spaniards
Sri Lanka	Sri Lankans
Sudan	Sudanese
Sweden	Swedes
Switzerland	Swiss
Syria	Syrians
Tanzania	Tanzanians
Thailand	Thais
Tibet	Tibetans
Turkey	Turks
Uganda	Ugandans
United States of America	Americans
Venezuela	Venezuelans
Vietnam	Vietnamese
Wales	Welsh
West Indies	West Indians
Yugoslavia	Yugoslavs
Zambia	Zambians
Zimbabwe	Zimbabweans

Days / Months / Seasons / Planets

Days

Sunday	Thursday
Monday	Friday
Tuesday	Saturday
Wednesday	

Months

January	July
February	August
March	September
April	October
May	November
June	December

Seasons

Spring	Autumn
Summer	Winter

Planets

Mercury	Mars	Uranus
Venus	Jupiter	Neptune
Earth	Saturn	Pluto

School work / Words in sums

School work

arithmetic	games	painting
art	geography	reading
dancing	history	science
drawing	music	writing

Words in sums

penny (1p)	inch (in)	millimetre (mm)
pound (£1.00)	foot (ft)	centimetre (cm)
	yard (yd)	metre (m)
		kilometre (km)

second (sec)	pint (pt)	litre (l)
minute (min)	quart (qt)	
hour (hr)	gallon (gal)	

ounce (oz)	gram (g)	half ($\frac{1}{2}$)
pound (lb)	kilogram (kg)	quarter ($\frac{1}{4}$)

abcdefghijklm
ABCDEFGHIJKLM